GUIDED READING BASICS

Organizing, managing, and implementing a balanced literacy program in K–3

Lori Jamison Rog

Stenhouse Publishers
PORTLAND, MAINE

Pembroke Publishers Limited
MARKHAM, ONTARIO

Dedication

My love and gratitude to Paul, who keeps me focused on the discipline and delight of writing.

This book is dedicated to my Reading Council and IRA colleagues, who continue to be my professional lifeline.

538 Hood Road
Markham, Ontario, Canada L3R 3K9
www.pembrokepublishers.com

Published in the U.S. by Stenhouse Publishers
477 Congress Street
Portland, ME 04101
www.stenhouse.com
Stenhouse ISBN 1-57110-383-X

We acknowledge the financial support of the Government of Canada through the Book Publishing Industry Development Program (BPIDP) for our publishing activities.

We acknowledge the Government of Ontario through the Ontario Media Development Corporation's Ontario Book Initiative.

Thanks to teacher Winnie Chiu and the students of Crescent Town P.S. featured on the cover.

National Library of Canada Cataloguing in Publication

Rog, Lori, 1955-
Guided reading basics / Lori Rog.

Includes bibliographical references and index.
For use in grades K-3.
ISBN 1-55138-160-5

1. Reading (Elementary) 2. Reading (Kindergarten) I. Title.

LB1525.77.G42 2003 372.4 C2003-902737-6

Editor: Kat Mototsune
Cover Design: John Zehethofer
Cover Photography: Ajay Photographics, PhotoDisk
Typesetting: Jay Tee Graphics Ltd.

Printed and bound in Canada
9 8 7 6 5 4 3 2 1

Contents

Introduction

When I began my career more than twenty years ago, teaching reading was much less complex than it is today. Back then, I had three reading groups, with students usually grouped as they had been the year before. I was provided with teacher's guides to tell me what and when to teach. And I had books full of seatwork to keep the students busy. Often with only one basal reader for all three groups, I had to slow things down and offer more skills practice for the weaker readers.

That simple teaching model had one major flaw: it didn't work for too many of the students. The three reading groups were too limiting and too inflexible to accommodate the increasingly wide range of students in my class. For the strong readers, the seatwork exercises were mindless time-fillers and the reading tasks offered little to extend their competency and maintain their interest. And by focusing on skills with my weaker readers, I was limiting the time they got to apply their learning to actual reading of books and stories. In effect, the kids who needed reading practice the most received the least practice in real reading!

A lot has changed over the past twenty years. Today, we know more about teaching and learning reading than ever before. We know that grouping must be flexible and constantly change to suit the learning needs of our students. We know that the texts used for teaching should offer just the right balance of support and challenge for each student. We know that the more kids read, the better readers they become. And we know that there is no single method of teaching that works for every child. Our students have different needs, different strengths, and different interests. And, in most classrooms, those differences are greater than they have ever been before.

A Guided Reading program is one way to help us meet the varied needs of all our students. Although Guided Reading may take different forms, the model I present in this book involves working with small groups of students at similar levels of development, using texts that are carefully matched to their needs, and providing instructional support to build reading strategies and increase independence.

Although reading instruction has traditionally involved guiding readers through texts, today's Guided Reading is different from traditional reading instruction in many ways.

We used to…	*But now we…*
…keep students in the same reading groups all year.	…constantly assess students' reading progress and regroup them accordingly.
…do all reading instruction with these groups.	…use ability grouping as just one aspect of the total language-arts program.

We used to…	*But now we…*
…choose stories for reading by theme, instinct, or "what came next in the basal reader."	…make educated decisions about reading materials at the appropriate levels of difficulty and interest for our students.
…select texts from a single basal reading program.	…use a variety of texts in a variety of genres.
…teach some students with texts that were too difficult for them to read and others with texts that were too easy.	…provide instruction using texts that are at each student's instructional reading level.
…focus on whether the student understood and remembered the story.	…focus on what the student has learned about being a strategic reader.
…place too much emphasis on after-reading activities.	…place more emphasis on before- and during-reading activities.
…ensure that students had lots of seatwork to keep them busy.	…teach students to independently engage in meaningful literacy activities.

The goal of today's Guided Reading is to nurture strategic, independent readers: as part of that goal, we form small, flexible groups of students with similar instructional needs; we select materials that provide just the right balance of support and challenge; and we scaffold the students as they develop the habits of independent, lifelong readers.

This book is intended both for teachers looking to implement a Guided Reading program in their classrooms, and for those who are looking to enhance their existing programs. All the tips and techniques in this book have been tried and tested in classrooms, and have proven effective in helping students become more proficient readers.

Chapters 1 to 4 lay the groundwork for organizing and managing a Guided Reading program. In Chapter 1, we look at how Guided Reading fits into the overall balanced literacy program. Chapters 2, 3, and 4 address the three key questions that teachers have about starting a Guided Reading program: how to organize the class for independent learning; how to select reading materials to meet the instructional needs of each group; and how to use assessment to group students.

Chapters 5 to 9 take a close look at the Guided Reading lesson itself, and how it differs at the emergent, early, developmental, and fluent reading levels. Chapters 10 to 14 discuss instruction strategies used in the Guided Reading program, including phonics, vocabulary study, comprehension strategies, retelling and responding to text, and the use of non-fiction in the Guided Reading program.

This book is intended to provide practical, classroom-tested strategies for organizing, managing, and implementing a Guided Reading program. But strategies are only as good as the teacher who implements them. There is no substitute for the knowledge and skill of an effective teacher. No textbook or teacher's guide can identify the needs and abilities of your students, and plan instruction to meet those needs. An effective Guided Reading program depends upon *you*.

This book is for beginning teachers who want to launch their careers with best practices in teaching reading. It is for experienced teachers who are constantly seeking to refine their craft. It is for all teachers who believe that Guided Reading is a tool in their pedagogical toolboxes that helps students build those important foundations of literacy.

Nobody said teaching was going to be easy. But it is my hope that this book will provide some tools and techniques to make the transition to Guided Reading instruction smoother and more efficient.

1 Guided Reading in the Balanced Literacy Program

Today, "balance" is the buzzword in literacy instruction. We work to *balance* a wide repertoire of teaching strategies and learning activities to meet the needs of all our students. We look for a *balance* of text resources, from picture books and novels, to newspaper articles and brochures, to posters and visuals. We strive to *balance* different grouping structures in our classrooms—whole-class, small-group, and individual. A balanced program requires opportunities for reading and writing *to* students, reading and writing *with* students, and reading and writing *by* students.

Guided Reading is only one component of the total balanced literacy program, but it is a very important one. As Dorothy Strickland suggests,

> Avoiding instructional extremes is at the heart of providing a balanced program of reading instruction…. However, finding the balance should not imply that there is a specific balanced approach. Nor should it suggest a sampling method in which "a little of this and a little of that" are mixed together to form a disparate grouping of approaches euphemistically termed "eclectic." Ultimately, instruction must be informed by how children learn and how they can best be taught. (Strickland, 1998, p. 52)

If you're starting to feel like a circus act, balancing spinning plates on a stick, it may help to think about your balanced literacy program as consisting of three blocks: the reading workshop, the writing workshop, and word study.

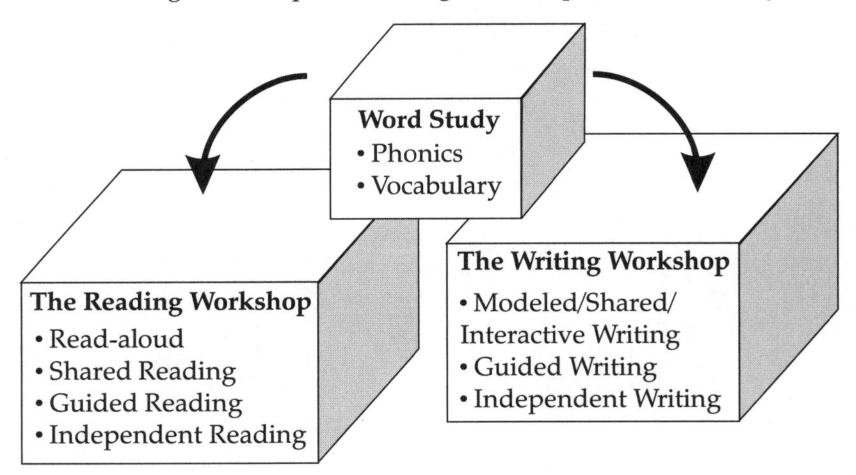

The Writing Workshop

Modeled, Shared, and Interactive Writing

The writing workshop starts with instruction through modeled, shared, and interactive writing.

Modeled writing is "writing out loud." The teacher demonstrates the processes involved in generating ideas and putting them down on paper, talking all the while about what she is thinking and doing. This is writing *for* students.

Shared writing involves the students in generating ideas for writing; for example, a language experience chart or a collaborative letter of thanks to the bus driver. The teacher is the scribe, talking about her writing process as the students contribute their ideas to the text. This is writing *with* students.

Interactive writing invites students to participate in the writing by "sharing the pen." The teacher guides a student who is writing, while other students observe and learn from the demonstration.

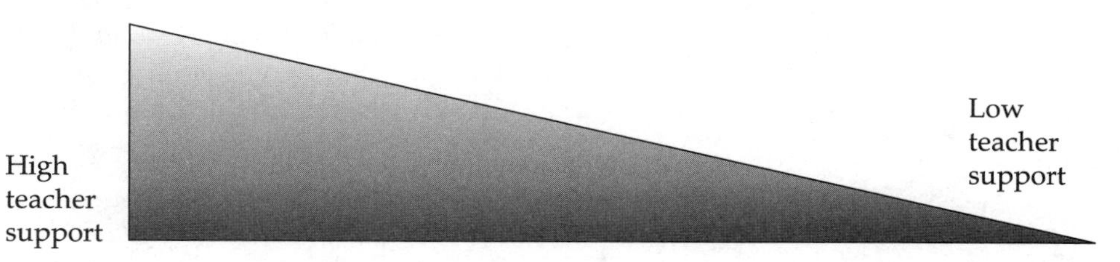

Modeled Writing—>Shared Writing—>Interactive Writing—>Guided Writing—>Independent Writing

Guided Writing

Guided writing provides support for students as they practise their skills and knowledge. It may take a variety of forms, such as small group writing, patterned writing, or guided revision.

- Small group writing activities may involve working in pairs to respond to a prompt or complete a writing task.
- Patterned writing provides a support to build confidence and teach written language structures. Stories may be patterned after read-alouds such as *Brown Bear, Brown Bear* by Bill Martin Jr. or *The Important Book* by Margaret Wise Brown. Or they may take the form of "fractured fairy tales," in which students rewrite a traditional tale changing one aspect of the story, such as setting, perspective, or ending.
- Guided revision requires students to revisit an existing draft and make focused improvements, such as highlighting tired, overused words and replacing them with more powerful vocabulary.

Donna Koch likes to use a Hello, Good-bye pattern as a guided writing activity to introduce a theme on the winter season. In a two-column chart, she brainstorms with the students a list of things they say good-bye to and a list of things they say hello to in winter. She models the creation from the list of a group poem called "Good-bye, Hello." Here is a recent example of her Grade 2 students' class poem:

Good-bye, Fall.
Hello, Winter.
Good-bye, colored leaves
Hello, sparkly snowflakes.
Good-bye, football
Hello, hockey.
Hello, Winter.
Good-bye, Fall.

Donna invites the students to work in pairs or individually to create "Good-bye, Hello" poems. Students can add this pattern to their writing folders if they wish to write similar poems on their own.

Independent Writing

Tip

Make your Author's Chair a celebration. Decorate a plastic lawn chair with ribbons, bows, and important words, and use it only for reading student writing aloud.

Independent writing is essential for students to practise the skills and strategies they have learned. Including both teacher-assigned and self-selected writing tasks, independent writing should incorporate opportunities for students to get responses to their writing—such as individual conferences and Author's Chair, in which students share their writing to receive feedback from others in the class. As part of this process, all students should be taught how to respond positively and constructively to the writing of others. This element of the writing workshop is important in that it validates all children's writing and builds students' confidence in themselves as writers.

Word Study

Tip

Teach students to "stretch" words like an elastic band, so they can hear every sound and represent each sound with a letter. Have students practise by using their hands to simulate the stretching as they say each sound of a word.

Word study is smallest of the three blocks because, as well as being a separate component of the balanced literacy program, it is also integrated into the reading and writing workshops. When we tell students to "stretch out the sounds" to spell a word, or talk about alternatives to tired words such as "nice" or "said," we are teaching word study. When we teach students to decode new words by making analogies to familiar words, or introduce key vocabulary words before reading, we are teaching word study. The word study block includes activities such as a High-frequency Word Wall or word play, but the learning should always be connected to reading or writing. Think of it as a whole–part–whole sequence: you pull the individual words or concepts from connected reading or writing experiences, study the pattern, then apply it in an authentic reading or writing situation.

The National Reading Panel's meta-analysis of reading research in the United States determined that systematic phonics instruction is one of the key elements in beginning reading. However, contrary to some interpretations of the NRP summary, the actual report of the panel stated that no single teaching approach is superior to any other. Your literacy program should include a *balance* of synthetic (blending sounds into words), analytic (separating words into sounds), and analogic (applying patterns from known to unknown) instruction.

See Chapter 11 for an extensive discussion of Word Study in the Guided Reading program.

The Reading Workshop

The reading workshop block has four components—interactive read-aloud, shared reading, guided reading, and independent reading—that represent decreasing levels of teacher support and student independence.

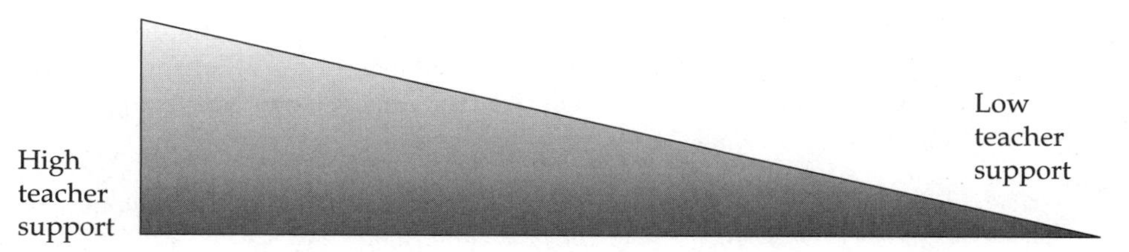

Interactive Read-aloud—>Shared Reading—>Guided Reading—>Independent Reading

Interactive Read-aloud

The interactive read-aloud is an opportunity for teachers to model reading fluency and strategies, and to expose students to books, ideas, and words that are beyond their current reading levels. When children listen to stories being read aloud, they gain experience with many forms and genres of writing. They extend their vocabulary, learn about story structure, and enrich their experience banks.

Three keys to an effective classroom read-aloud program are

- selecting high-quality fiction and non-fiction that extends children's knowledge of literature, language, and the world
- active participation by children that constructs knowledge and extends thinking
- rereading familiar texts to reinforce children's knowledge of the reading process and how language goes together

Tip

Your read-aloud program should include many books that are "old friends." Revisiting familiar texts is of major importance.

Shared Reading

Shared reading may be described as "learning to read by reading." Using a large text that is visible to all, the teacher demonstrates the use of reading strategies, allowing the students observe and join in. As the text is read and reread several times, students read chorally with the teacher when they become familiar with the text. During these readings, the teacher may focus on concepts about print, story structure, or text features such as rhymes, letter patterns, and punctuation.

Although any text may be used for shared reading, certain genres like rhymes, songs, and predictable stories are excellent choices. Big books, language experience charts, and pocket charts are often used. Again, it is important to give students experiences with a variety of text forms, including non-fiction and poetry. Shared reading enables students to participate in reading texts that are beyond their reading levels. More importantly, it accommodates a variety of levels of development, as each child gains something different from the experience.

Guided Reading

Guided Reading scaffolds, or supports, young readers as they negotiate texts and develop independent reading strategies.

There are several key characteristics of Guided Reading:

Scaffolding involves providing supports for learners that enable them to become increasingly independent.

- **working with groups of no more than 4 to 6 students**
  When teachers work with small groups, they are able to identify the strategies each child is using and what instruction is needed. Group interaction enables students to learn from one another and helps them take their thinking to a higher level.
- **using texts at the instructional level of the students in the group**
  The text should be chosen to provide just the right balance of challenge and support—easy enough for students to read most of the story with the strategies they have, but challenging enough to require some strategy use.
- **focusing on the reading strategies students need at that point in their development**
  Guided Reading instruction focuses on what the students need to know, rather than what a textbook says should come next. It provides instruction in response to student needs, not according to a pre-set program.
- **frequent and consistent monitoring of progress**
  Running records, anecdotal notes, informal observations, and other assessments help teachers determine what students know and can do, and what they need to learn next.
- **keeping the groups flexible and dynamic**
  Students are placed in groups according to their reading levels and strategy use, as determined by the teacher's ongoing assessments. Groups change as students grow.
- **striving to build independent, fluent readers**
  The instructional focus is on reading strategies, not just questions and activities around a particular text.

There are three main steps to organizing your Guided Reading program:

1. *Establish routines and procedures for independent learning.*
2. *Gather a collection of books and other texts, organized by levels of difficulty and supports for the reader.*
3. *Assess your students to determine instructional reading levels and to establish groups.*

Children who are learning to read need a balance of literacy experiences, learning activities, grouping structures, and reading genres. Guided Reading enables teachers to help students develop the strategies required for independent reading.

Independent Reading

Like independent writing, independent reading provides students with opportunities to practise reading strategies, develop fluency, and build lifelong reading habits. There is substantial research linking the amount of recreational reading with reading proficiency. An effective independent reading program requires time for reading as well as books that students will be able to read with ease and enjoy. Because emergent-level texts may not be available at libraries and bookstores, you will want to ensure that your students have opportunities to borrow texts at the appropriate level from your classroom library.

Fitting It All In

For most teachers, it is not the individual components of the literacy program that are challenging; it is fitting them together in a cohesive framework that promotes student engagement and achievement. Of course, the instructional routines and procedures you establish in your classroom will vary according to your own teaching style, the needs of your students, and the learning objectives you establish for them. However, a consistent routine supports student learning and enhances the classroom climate. For increasing numbers of your students, school may provide the only structure in their lives. The fact that they know what to expect when they arrive in your classroom each day helps to create a safe and orderly learning environment for them.

Tip

Make a point of putting the books used for shared reading and read-aloud in the classroom library. These will be favorite choices for free-time reading.

Heather Wilson, who teaches a combined Grade 1 and 2 classroom, sets up her literacy schedule in this way:

As students arrive in the classroom, they know to select a book and read or browse until it is time for the shared literacy experiences. In her inner city school, where many of the children drift in after the morning bell, Heather believes that this routine, which includes books and a breakfast snack, will encourage punctuality in her students.

When the morning procedures, such as attendance and agendas, are complete, Heather begins her literacy workshop. Depending on her learning objectives, she will begin with shared writing, shared reading, or read-aloud. A language experience activity can serve as both shared reading and shared or interactive writing. Sometimes she will use this time for the daily read-aloud of a piece of literature or non-fiction that matches both the theme she is teaching and the learning objectives she has selected for her students. Because this is whole-class learning time, she must ensure that these activities provide multiple levels of learning.

Following the shared literacy workshop, the students engage in independent learning routines while Heather works with small needs-based groups for Guided Reading instruction. Heather spent several weeks at the beginning of the school year establishing the routines and procedures for independent learning, so that she could work uninterrupted with her Guided Reading groups. Even now, she finds it most expedient to work with one group before recess and one group after recess, as many of her students are still not able to remain engaged in independent activities for forty minutes at a time.

Following the recess break, Heather may reassemble the Guided Reading groups, read aloud to the class, or move right into the writing workshop. She strives to provide a balance (there's that word again!) of student self-selected writing, teacher assignments, and journals and learning logs. The writing workshop always begins with a short lesson, which may take the form of modeled or interactive writing, or may be literature related. And it always ends with a sharing opportunity during Author's Chair.

Many of Heather's students come from families in distress, poverty, abuse, and a host of other issues. Because they know that when they come to school there will be predictable routines, they will experience success, be supported by their teacher, and make achievements against the odds.

Heather Wilson's Literacy Timetable

Time	*Literacy Activity*	*Texts/Materials*	*Grouping Structure*
9:00	Book Browsing: students select a book for independent reading or browsing, and gather on the carpet until everyone is assembled and lessons can begin.	Self-selected independent-reading materials	Individual or buddies
9:15	Shared Literacy Routines: shared reading *or* modeled, shared, or interactive writing	• Big Books, Interactive, or Language experience • Chart paper	Whole class (built-in structures mean learning can take place at many levels)
9:30 9:45 10:00	Guided Reading: 2–3 groups per day Independent Literacy Routines	Leveled reading materials at instructional level of groups; balance of fiction and non-fiction	Small, needs-based groups Heterogeneous groups or individual
10:15	Word Wall Routines	High-frequency words "harvested" from reading and writing	Whole class or large group, as needed
10:30	Recess Break		
10:45	Interactive Read-aloud	Well written texts in a variety of genres; beyond students' reading level	Whole class
11:00 11:15 11:30	Writing Workshop • mini lesson • independent writing • Author's Chair	Writing materials; writing may extend from read-aloud	Individual
11:45	Lunch		

Weekly Timetable

Theme: Names

Monday	*Tuesday*	*Wednesday*	*Thursday*	*Friday*
Book Browsing	Book Browsing	Book Browsing	Book Browsing	Book Browsing
Word Wall: *said, they*	Word Wall: *with, of*	Word Wall: review	Word Wall: *keep, put*	Word Wall: review
Buzz Groups: students talk to buddies about how they were named	Shared Writing: Name Poems (acrostics)	Shared Reading: S. Silverstein poem; reread to enjoy rhythm, rhyme, meaning	Revisit yesterday's poem to examine text features: rhyme, spelling	Big Book: *The Name of the Tree*
Modeled writing: lang-exp. chart Shared reading: lang-exp. chart	Reread yesterday's chart	Modeled writing: revising and editing Name Poem		
Guided Reading: Group 1 (Em) Group 3 (Er1) Group 5 (Fl)	Guided Reading: Group 1 Group 2 (Er2) Group 4 (D)	Guided Reading: Group 3 "catch-up"	Guided Reading: Group 1 Group 3 Group 5	Guided Reading: Group 1 Group 2 Group 4
Interactive Read-aloud: *Chrysanthemum*	Interactive Read-aloud: *Matthew ABC*	Interactive Read-aloud: revisit *Chrysanthemum*	Interactive Read-aloud: *The Name Jar*	Interactive Read-aloud: revisit book of students' choice
Writing Workshop: week-end journals	Writing Workshop: Name Poems	Writing Workshop: illustrate and "publish" Name Poems	Writing Workshop: free choice	Writing Workshop: book response of reader's choice

2 Establishing Independent Learning Routines

"Okay, it's easy to work with a group of four students, but what do I do with the rest of them?"

The first concern of many teachers when setting up a Guided Reading program is organizing and managing the classroom so that all students are engaged in productive learning experiences, whether they are working directly with the teacher or not.

The ultimate goal of education is to teach students to be independent learners. Teaching students to work on their own and in groups, solving their own problems and taking responsibility for their own learning, is one of the teacher's most important tasks. We are doing our students no favors when we unintentionally teach them to look to us for direction in everything they do.

Literacy centres are not the only way to engage students in independent learning. Other strategies include independent reading time, teacher-assigned activities, guided literacy groups under the direction of a support teacher or paraprofessional, and self-selected learning. When we are aware of alternatives, we can establish the routines that work best for ourselves and for our students. Whatever learning activities we choose, however, it is vital that they contribute to making the students better readers, writers, and thinkers.

Independent Reading Time

Research has demonstrated a strong correlation between students' reading proficiency and the quantity of independent reading they do. Whether this means that good readers just read more, or that more reading makes you a better reader, the implications are clear: We need to ensure that our students have many opportunities to practise reading using a variety of texts.

Lucy Calkins, in *The Art of Teaching Reading* (2001), expresses concern that today's students lack reading stamina, the ability to sustain attention to reading for lengths of time. But even the youngest students can be taught to interact with books for 20 minutes or more. It should be noted, however, that in the Kindergarten or beginning Grade 1 classroom, uninterrupted, sustained, silent reading is unlikely to be silent, uninterrupted, or, for that matter, even reading!

Connie Watson, a Grade 1 teacher in an urban school, begins each school year by teaching her students Ways to Read in Grade 1. She carefully models different approaches to interacting with texts: "Sometimes we just look at the pictures and think about them. Sometimes we make up our own story to go along with the pictures. Sometimes we can read some of the words in the story."

As a result of Connie's careful preparations early the year, she never has a student say, "But I don't know how to read." In spite of the fact that her students come to school without a rich background in literacy, she is able to validate their interactions with books and demonstrate how to make effective use of school reading time.

You may be surprised at how long your students will be able to remain engaged in books. I remember teaching a particularly energetic Grade 2 class a few years ago. After clearly laying out my expectations for independent reading time, I set a timer for two minutes and explained that they would not be able to leave their chosen reading spot or choose a new book until the timer went off. Gradually I increased the amount of time on the timer until, by the end of the year, they complained that I was cutting their reading period short if I set the timer for less than 20 minutes!

Routines and procedures for independent reading are as important as any other aspect of classroom instruction. At first, mini lessons may include how to select an appropriate book. Jeff Ruf, a teacher librarian, uses the Five Finger Rule to help students find books that are just right for them (see BLM page 19). The Five Finger Rule teaches students that if there are five words they don't know on a single page, then the book is probably too hard for them.

Books for independent reading should be at a reader's independent reading level; in other words, they should be able to read virtually every word and comprehend thoroughly.

That's not to say that children can't ever appreciate books that are beyond their own reading levels, especially if they are highly motivated. We all know children who are so desperate to read a special dinosaur book or the latest fantasy everyone is talking about that they will struggle through the text, no matter how difficult it is. However, both research and best practice suggest that students should be able to read independent-level text with at least 95% accuracy and thorough comprehension. Books for independent reading should be at a reader's independent reading level; in other words, they should be able to read virtually every word and understand completely. Teachers and parents sometimes assume that a reader needs to be challenged in their reading. But independent reading should be easy. Challenging reading should be read aloud or saved for instructional purposes, when the teacher can scaffold the students through the reading.

Buddy Reading

Reading with partners is a great way to build reading fluency and to practise. Students may read from the same book or from books of their individual choice. Heather Garbutt developed the Nine P's Reading poster found on page 19 to give her students some guidelines, and to help her students practise, present, and praise their reading. Nine P's Reading is just one buddy-reading routine that may be used during independent reading time.

Student Accountability in Independent Reading

Many teachers struggle with the level of accountability expected of students in their independent reading program. To what extent should we require students to respond to their reading experiences? Or should we allow them to enjoy the independent reading experience without additional responsibility? There are arguments on behalf of both.

The use of response journals or reading logs adds an element of accountability. As teachers, we can be more confident that our students actually have read what they say they have read. We get a sense of how much they understand, and hope that they have extended their thinking to a higher level.

On the other hand, the task of responding to every piece of reading can be annoying to our most prolific readers, and even more limiting to our reluctant readers. And every minute spent responding is a minute taken away from actually reading.

Tip

Using an Independent Reading Record, we can learn about the student's reading choices, his or her perceptions of self as a reader, and the quantity of reading the student is doing.

A simple reading log such as the Independent Reading Record on page 20 enables the teacher to learn a great deal about a student's reading habits without burdening the reader too much.

Regardless of how we choose to organize independent reading time, it is important for teachers to think carefully about our purposes for *all* learning activities, and remind ourselves that any tasks we assign our students must help them to become more proficient readers, writers, or thinkers.

Teacher-assigned Activities

Assigning reading or writing activities is a perfectly legitimate way to engage our students while we are occupied with other groups. Sometimes we want them to undertake a pre-reading activity in preparation for the Guided Reading lesson ahead; sometimes they will be completing a piece of reading or an extension activity from a previous Guided Reading lesson.

For example, in preparation for the reading of a fluent-level text on spiders, the teacher provides the students in the group with an anticipation guide—a set of statements about spiders that the group must discuss and identify as true or false. This will establish a context for the reading when they come to the Guided Reading lesson. After the lesson, they may be asked to complete the reading of the text or use the information in the story to create a riddle book on spiders. Again this may be done during independent work time.

Sometimes assigned activities will be completed individually, at other times in pairs or small groups. Whatever the assignment, it is important that the students understand what is expected of them, both in terms of learning and behavior. The teacher must not be interrupted from the Guided Reading group to answer questions or clarify assignments.

Students who are accustomed to working in groups learn quickly how to ask one another for help, and how to provide help appropriately. If help is not available, they must learn to move on to something else rather than getting blocked at the point of misunderstanding. Even those who use the "ask three, then me" routine know that the teacher may not always be available at the moment of need. Here are some routines to suggest to students for seeking help while the teacher is occupied:

- Establish a student expert of the day to answer questions on that topic. This student might be identified by a special badge or armband.
- *3 B4 Me* and "Ask three, then me" are reminders to students that they should seek help from three peers before waiting until the teacher is free to respond.
- Students place yellow cards on the corner of their desks to signal that they need help when the teacher is available. They move on to something else until the teacher can help them.

Five Finger Rule!

1. Open your book to the middle
2. Open up your hand.
3. Read a page of the book to yourself
4. Put down one finger each time you find a tricky word.
5. If your thumb is still up at the end of the page, it is probably a good book for you!

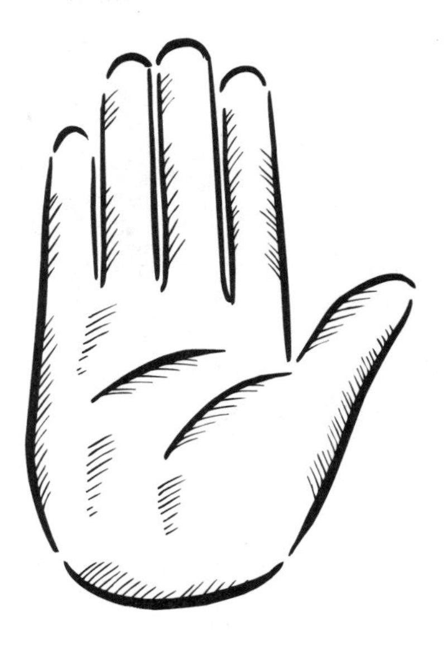

Nine P's Reading

1. **P**ick a book.
2. **P**ractise reading it.
3. **P**ick a partner.
4. **P**lan how you and your partner will read.
5. **P**lace yourselves hip to hip so you can both see the books.
6. **P**resent your reading of the book or part of the book to your partner.
7. **P**olitely listen to your partner read.
8. **P**raise each other's reading.
9. **P**ut your books away where they belong.

Independent Reading Record

Title and Author	*Pages*	*Genre*	*Did you finish it?*	*Did you like it?*	*Have you read it before?*	*Easy, Medium, or Hard?*	*Read at home or school?*
Amelia Bedelia By Peggy Parrish	48	Fiction	yes	yes	no	E	H

As with any routine, this process must be modeled, taught, and practised before the students can be expected to function independently.

Explicitly show the students what you expect of their behavior and work habits. Guide them in the practice of the routine before expecting them to engage in it on their own.

Guided Literacy Groups

If you are fortunate enough to have paraprofessional and professional support in your school, you might establish guided literacy groups. In guided literacy groups, students move with their needs-based groupings to various literacy activities, ranging from interactive writing to word study, all directed by a teacher or paraprofessional.

McDermid School in Regina is one school where literacy groups are working successfully, to the extent that this school was recognized as having an Exemplary Reading Program by the International Reading Association.

All Grade 1 students are assessed early in the school year, and are divided into five or more needs-based literacy groups. Then classroom teacher Bonnie Banting works on Guided Reading with one group while reading specialist Mary Ann Sjogren Branch guides an interactive writing session. Other groups include a speech-language pathologist working on phonological awareness and the teacher-librarian presenting a read-aloud experience. The remaining groups work with various paraprofessionals who supervise oral reading practice or programmed word study.

McDermid School Model

Classroom Teacher	Guided Reading
Learning Assistance Teacher	Interactive Writing
Speech-Language Pathologist	Phonological Awareness
Teacher-Librarian	Read-aloud and Literature Activity
Paraprofessionals	Phonics and Word Study Activities

At McDermid School, the literacy groups program runs three days a week, for 90 minutes each session. During this time the students cycle through three different learning stations. The rest of the time, the students are involved in a balanced literacy program in their own classroom.

The entire team, including the principal, meets weekly to discuss the students and determine whether groups need to be adjusted, which students to move ahead, and which may need additional intervention.

While the McDermid School model requires a high degree of organization and cooperation from all members of the teaching staff, teachers report that it is well worth the time and effort. In spite of the fact that many students in this inner-city school come to school without a rich literacy background, few students require intervention beyond Grade 1. The special attention to reading and writing at the outset pays off, in students who progress through the grades with a firm literacy foundation.

Other schools are working with variations of this arrangement that suit their own particular needs. The common elements are that students are placed in needs-based groupings for part of the language arts program, and all are receiving instruction and materials appropriate to their needs from a caring and capable adult.

It has been said that "it takes a village to raise a child." Certainly this initiative lives up to the philosophy that it takes a whole school to help a child become literate.

Self-selected Learning

Teaching students to make decisions about their own learning is one of the most important responsibilities teachers have. Project-based learning is one way students can learn to make choices, work independently, organize their own time, and solve their own problems. Experts in differentiated instruction inform us that involving students in choosing, monitoring, and assessing their own learning contributes to maximizing their growth as learners (Tomlinson, 1999).

Projects are one way to engage students in independent learning. A project can take different forms: it might be written research and reporting on a topic of interest; it might be a multimedia display; it might involve responding to literature through the arts. Involving students in independent projects helps them learn to organize their time and guide their own learning, while enabling them to focus on areas of individual strength and interest.

Choice menus provide students with a specific range of activities. They might involve choosing from

- a range of texts on a particular topic or by the same author. After reading, the students complete an assignment, such as writing a report or a response. There may be a standard assignment, or an assignment tucked into each book.
- several response or extension options to reading, such as writing, drawing, or creative dramatics (see page 24)
- a variety of alternatives for reading, ranging from reading a classroom Big Book to reading along with a tape (see example on page 25).

Some choice menus may offer activities at different levels of difficulty, to accommodate different student needs and interests. For example, the choice menu on Spiders on page 26 asks students to complete one item from each row. The top row contains visual art options, the middle row contains oral reading options, and the bottom row contains writing options. The choices in each row are graduated from easy to difficult.

The gathering grid (see page 27) is a tool for organizing information about a topic. Students list two or three questions along the left side of the grid, and then collect notes from different texts to respond to the questions. This teaches even our youngest researchers to use different sources for gathering information.

If students are to be evaluated on their participation in the choice menu, it is important that timelines and expectations be made very clear to them at the outset. A contract format enables students to direct their own learning, and helps differentiate expectations for different students. Students can work with you to create their own contracts, or you might give a minimum set of expectations. For example, some students may be expected to read three books on a list, while others may read five or six. You are the best judge of how to challenge each student without overwhelming him or her.

Literacy Centres

Literacy centres are areas within the classroom where students work alone or together to explore literacy activities. Learning centres should provide ideas and materials that will help move students away from teacher-dominated learning and toward self-selected learning.

Some teachers have been led to believe that literacy centres are the only independent learning routine for a Guided Reading program. This is not so! Literacy centres are only one way of organizing your classroom for independent learning, but it can be a very effective one if you organize the centres carefully and take time to teach the routines and procedures.

Literacy centres lend themselves ideally to word study activities: manipulating magnetic letters, prefixes, and suffixes on the overhead projector; word-family games. This is both an advantage and a disadvantage. At the closing general session of the 2002 International Reading Association Convention, Regie Routman, author of *Literacy at the Crossroads* and other professional books for teachers, expressed a concern that the students she observed in literacy centres were often spending very little time engaged in connected reading. A caution for teachers establishing literacy centres is to ensure that students experience a balance of literacy activities, including reading texts of different genres and writing in a variety of forms.

Another misconception about literacy centres is that they require a lot of space and elaborate display. A container of pointers for reading around the room can be considered a centre. A placemat, a square tablecloth, or even a hula hoop can define space for a centre. A backpack, pencil box, or basket can contain a portable centre that may be taken to a student's own work space.

Tip

Expert teachers advise that having 10 to 12 centre options in place will ensure that students have plenty of choice and no centre will have too many children in it at once.

Generally speaking, it is not necessary to change centres too frequently. Most will remain in place all year, with only the artifacts changing to suit the changing needs of the students.

Additional key points about literacy centres:

- Not all literacy centres will be product-based; in many cases, the focus will be the learning process. For example, activities like reading around the room, buddy reading, or reading along with a tape will have no accountability process in place. They require the students to focus on reading practice, along with effective habits of managing time, making choices, and using resources wisely.
- Ideally, the activities in the literacy centre should be varied and open-ended, so that the students will have opportunities for both success and challenge.
- Activities should accommodate a variety of ability levels and provide some student choice. They may provide students with an opportunity to explore an area of interest or to practise a previously taught skill or strategy.

Clear and explicit management is the key to success with literacy centres. "You are teaching more than literacy. You are helping children understand how to conduct themselves as members of cooperative groups. They are learning how to fulfill commitments, manage time, manage tasks without constant reminders and supervision, conserve materials, collaborate with others, and respect others' rights." (Fountas and Pinnell, 1996, page 65)

Choice Menu: Reading Activity Bingo

Read a book of your choice and complete any row of activities—across, up and down, or corner to corner.

Practise reading with lots of expression. **Read out loud** to a buddy. Have your buddy sign this box when you're done.	Write a **new story** using the same characters.	Do a **word hunt** in your book for fifteen words of your choice. Write them on cards and sort them into groups. Explain how you sorted them.
Choose one thing from the story and write an **informational report** about it.	Write a **review** of this book, telling other readers if you would recommend it and why.	Make a **story map** with pictures and words telling what happened in your book.
Write a **"telephone poem"** about the story, using the digits in your phone number.	Make puppets of your book characters and **act out the story** for a friend. Practise first!	**Rewrite** the same story, changing one character, event or setting.

Choice Menu: Things to do During Reading Time

Name: ______________________ *Week of:* ______________________

Color in a box each time you complete an activity.

Activity									
Choose a pointer and read around the room									
Read from your book basket									
Read a book to a buddy									
Read a big book									
Read one of our theme books									
Read an ABC book									
Read one of our class books									
Read from the poem box									
Read an information book									
Read a book on the computer									
Read a book with a tape									

Sample Choice Menu

Please read three books from the Spider theme box and select one activity from each row to complete.

Row 1	*Row 2*	*Row 3*
Create an illustration for one part of the book.	Draw a picture of a spider and label all its parts	Make three pictures and add captions to describe three facts about spiders.
Practise reading one paragraph or page and read it aloud to a friend.	Read one of the books with a friend. Each of you take turns reading one page at a time.	Practise reading a page out loud and present it to the class with lots of expression.
Write three interesting facts you learned about spiders.	Write three things you know about spiders and three things you would like to find out.	Write a one-page report on spiders.

Choice Menu: Gathering Grid

Think of three things you would like to find out about your topic. Write them as questions in the squares. Then read three books on the topic. Under each title, list any facts you learned in answer to your question.

	Book #1 *Title and Author*	*Book #2* *Title and Author*	*Book #3* *Title and Author*
Question #1			
Question #2			
Question #3			

Centre Rotation Models

There are several ways to organize your classroom for students to rotate through centres. Using standard rotation, the teacher assigns each group to an initial centre, then groups rotate through the centres on a prescribed schedule.

Standard Rotation Schedule

Time	*Blue Group*	*Yellow Group*	*Red Group*	*Green Group*
9:20–9:40	Teacher Group	Writing	Reading	Creative Activities
9:40–10:00	Creative Activities	Teacher Group	Writing	Reading
10:00–10:20	Reading	Creative Activities	Teacher Group	Writing
10:20–10:40	Writing	Reading	Creative Activities	Teacher Group

Tip

Limit the number of students at a centre at any given time. Behavior problems often occur when there are too many people at a centre. Some teachers suggest that two or three children to a centre is optimal, depending on the age of the students and the nature of the work.

In the free-choice model, students decide which centres they choose to go to. There may or may not be a specified time limit. Although some teachers may be uncomfortable with this arrangement at first, most students become quite competent at self-regulating centre visits, once routines and procedures are established.

Teachers have different ways of managing the independent selection of centre. Usually, centre time begins with an opportunity for students to sign up for the centre of their choice by placing their name cards in a small pocket chart with the names of the centres on the pockets. Some teachers prefer to allow students the independence to decide when to move from centre to centre. This means students may choose to stay at one centre for the entire time, or to move to an open centre when they are done. It also opens up the possibility of some students monopolizing popular centres like the computer, and this issue must be dealt with in the classroom routines. Other teachers prefer to limit the time students may spend at one centre, monitoring centre time with a timer. In this situation, students need to sign up for two or more centres each day, depending on the length of the centre time.

Also popular is the assignment model, in which the teacher determines some or all of the centres each student must visit. For example, the teacher might require that students *must* visit the Browsing Boxes and the Writing Corner, but *may* also visit other centres that interest them, as time permits. In this way, the teacher can differentiate literacy centre requirements for different students.

Another structure is to require all students to visit all centres in the course of a week, but the students themselves can decide on the order and timing. Some sort of tracking form is necessary to monitor which centres have been visited. Some teachers use a chart or a picture on which the children mark one element for each centre visited. You might want to have a four-day cycle, with Fridays designated as catch-up days for students to visit centres they did not complete or would like to revisit.

Tip

Colored hairbands are inexpensive (and washable!) placeholders for literacy centres.

Ideally, centre groups should be heterogeneous and flexible. This means that students may be pulled from a variety of centres for Guided Reading instruction. The use of bracelets, necklaces, or other placeholders enable a student to return to the same centre after Guided Reading time: students choosing to work at that centre put on one of the color-coded bracelets there to designate their spot in that centre, and return the bracelet when they are done to indicate that someone else may have a spot at the centre.

A Dozen Dynamic Literacy Centres

It is not necessary to change centres every week or every month. Many of your centres may be available all year long, with new materials or activities added on a regular basis. Here are some popular literacy centres to consider:

1. Reading Around the Room
This centre consists of merely a collection of pointers and framers for students to use as they walk around the classroom and read all the environmental print they can find. Many teachers have highly creative collections of tracking tools, but even chopsticks or wooden dowels with a dab of colored paint or nail polish at the end work very well. A fly swatter with a square cut out of the middle can serve as an effective tool for framing words around the room.

2. Buddy Reading or Independent Reading
Reading practice should be an essential element of any independent learning activity. Students may choose from the classroom library, student-made books, and theme books, or you may direct them to choose texts from a book basket at their independent reading level. Independent reading practice may be individual or with a partner.

3. Reading Overhead Transparencies
Set an overhead projector on the floor to project on the wall or on a piece of chart paper mounted on the wall. The options for this centre are unlimited. Students may read poems and stories on transparencies (stored in plastic sheet protectors) or they can sequence cut-up stories. They might highlight features of print, such as high-frequency words or consonant blends. Or they might write their own stories on the overhead.

4. Pocket-chart Reading
Allow students to manipulate sentence strips and words in the pocket chart. Have them sort poems and stories that have been read in shared reading. They might also use the pocket chart for word sorts and practice in alphabetical order.

Tip

The Word Work Centre is an excellent place to reinforce words from the classroom Word Wall. One activity is to create a set of cards with each of the high-frequency words that have been studied: the students draw two cards and try to keep a tally of how many times they find the words in a page from a newspaper or magazine. It doesn't matter if they can't read the newspaper page; the key is that they can recognize the designated high-frequency words.

5. Read-along/Listening Centre
Many classrooms have a listening post where students listen and read along with stories, poems, and songs on tape. Individual portable cassette recorders may also be purchased very inexpensively. Ask parents to help with taping stories; children will love to hear their own parents' voices in the school room! Students themselves also enjoy taping and listening to their own reading.

6. Computer Centre
Use the classroom computers with appropriate software, such as interactive storybooks or writing programs. E-books are also becoming available for even the youngest readers.

7. Word Work Centre
There are many ways students can work on spelling and language activities, using plastic letters, letter cards or tiles, alphabet books, and other manipulatives. Metal cookie sheets or stovetop burner protectors may be used with magnetic

letters. Individual whiteboards can be made by cutting a sheet of white laminate into 30-cm squares (sometimes a lumber yard will do this for you). Word games to reinforce rimes (see page 87) and onsets, and high-frequency word activities are important components of this kind of centre.

8. Writing Centre

The writing centre should be filled with many sizes, colors, and types of paper and plenty of tools for writing. Some teachers also include stamps and stickers. Seasonal notepaper may be provided. Word Walls and dictionaries are valuable resources. Include a bulletin board or Writer's Wall—a whiteboard where students can share "million-dollar words" or great writing ideas.

9. Message Centre

This is a place where students can write messages to one another or to other people. A list of all the students' names, along with photocopies of their pictures, would be helpful to young writers. Sentence stems to copy—such as "I hope you feel better" or "I'm sorry"—can be included. Samples of greeting cards and postcards also generate ideas. Of course, the students need some place to "mail" their letters. Milk cartons with the tops cut off or plastic shoe pockets that hang on the door can be turned into individual mailboxes.

10. "Letter" Centre

For emergent readers, this is an opportunity to sort and match letters and sounds. For example, they might sort pictures or objects that rhyme or start with the same sound. Students can practise their printing or handwriting, using magic slates or by tracing on plastic placemats decorated with the alphabet.

11. Discovery Centre

Birds' nests, seashells, animal teeth, rocks, and seeds of different kinds are just some of the scientific artifacts that might be placed at this centre, which is usually related to a theme you are studying in the class. Be sure to include literacy artifacts—such as informational books, brochures, and magazines—and materials for writing: labels, signs, directions, captions, and reports.

12. Story-telling Centre

This centre might contain a variety of puppets, props, and costumes. Books might be included as reminders for telling the story. Readers theatre scripts may also be made available.

Tips for Organizing and Managing Literacy Centres

- **Keep it Simple!** Maintain several permanent centres and just change a few activities and resources at a time.
- **Let the Kids Do It!** Set up the centres so that students can manage clean up and maintenance of the materials.
- **Look for Creative Storage Solutions!** Centres do not need to take up a lot of space. Some may be stored in baskets, racks, decorated gift bags, or even backpacks. An old wagon donated or purchased at a garage sale is great storage for a mobile centre.
- **Ring around the Centre!** Keep game cards and game boards together by punching a hole in the corner of the game board and each of the cards and attaching them together with a metal ring. Other game pieces may be stored in a resealable bag with a hole in the corner.

Teaching Routines and Procedures

Before you begin to pull small groups for instruction, it is essential to create the routines and procedures that will enable all your students to work productively, whether you are working with them or whether they are on their own.

Regardless of the independent learning routines you select, it is important to take as much time as needed to teach the routines and procedures. Guided Reading expert Helen Depree (1994) suggests that it takes six to eight weeks to establish the routines necessary to implement a Guided Reading program. As with any new concept or procedure, it is important to model and demonstrate what you want the students to do, then provide them with many opportunities for guided practice before expecting them to engage in these activities independently. "Every moment invested in teaching routines is time well spent, because it will save hours of instructional time later." (Fountas and Pinnell, 1996, p. 62)

Whether it is a learning centre, independent project, or other activity, it is important to introduce children to the routine one step at a time.

1. Model how to do the activity. Talk about why it is important or what a student learns from it. Explicitly teach what to do and what is expected in terms of learning activity and behavior.
2. Have one or two children demonstrate the activity at a time.
3. Ensure that all children have an opportunity for guided practice in the activity.
4. Allow students who are capable of working independently to start work at the centre or in the activity. Gradually allow others to join as they demonstrate ability to function independently.
5. Observe and wait until you are confident that children are using the activities independently and productively before introducing a new element.
6. Add new centres or activities one at a time. Introduce each one carefully and explicitly, and allow students opportunities to practise with support.
7. Teach students how to make the transition from one activity to another, and to put away the materials from one task before moving to another.

Tip

Take time to teach! It will probably take 6–8 weeks to get the routines and procedures in place to begin a Guided Reading program.

3 Choosing Materials for Guided Reading

Choosing and using texts that are appropriate for each group of students is one of the most important features of the Guided Reading program. Fortunately, you don't have to go out and purchase an elaborate set of resources. Start by taking an inventory of the materials you already have in your school and your classroom.

Which of these resources do you already have in your classroom?

- beginning readers
- trade picture books ("real" literature)
- novels and early chapter books
- series books
- literary anthologies
- basal readers
- informational books
- other print materials, such as charts and brochures
- poetry books

The good news is that every one of these can be used for Guided Reading. In fact, one of the goals of Guided Reading is to help our students develop strategies for reading all kinds of genres and text forms. In recent years we have seen a plethora of publishing in the field of early literacy, with texts carefully constructed to provide the supports that beginning readers need.

Readability

Each day, students should read two kinds of texts:

1. ***texts that they can read independently***
2. ***texts that offer enough challenge to be read with teacher or tutor support***

The most important consideration in book selection is not the topic, theme, or genre; it is the degree of difficulty for each student. For teaching purposes, we want texts in which the students will be able to read about nine out of ten words and have a basic understanding of what they read. This ensures that the reader will have enough success with the reading to gain the confidence to tackle the words and ideas that are challenging. The reader will be able to read most of the text, but will have to apply some reading strategies in order to access it completely.

Leveled Books

For reading instruction, leveled books are a convenient resource, but not essential. There are many sources of leveled lists available from publishers to help you level your own book collections. Check out *Guided Reading: Good First Teaching for All Students* and other books by Irene Fountas and Gay Su Pinnell for lists of hundreds of books. The Developmental Reading Assessment (DRA) is another system of leveling books for instruction. Most educational publishers today will provide you with the Fountas and Pinnell or DRA levels of their materials.

Leveled lists are a tool to make it easier for you to select materials at increasing levels of support for your students. When you have identified an appropriate book for a group of students, it is convenient to have access to a variety of other texts of equivalent difficulty. However, only you know your students and what kinds of texts will be most appropriate to meet their interests and learning needs. The ultimate decision about what books to use will have to come from your knowledge of your students, your books and the reading process.

When we talk about levels, we are really referring to the amount of challenge a text provides for the reader. Leveling a book involves evaluating the readability of the text and looking at its layout, design, and picture support.

Factors that influence the ease or difficulty with which a reader can access a particular text include

- *Amount, appearance, and placement of print on the page*
- *Predictability and support from illustrations*
- *Complexity of themes and concepts*
- *Complexity of language structures*

Calculating the readability of texts is not a new process. For almost 50 years, readability formulas such as the Fry Chart or the Flesch-Kincaid Graph have used mathematical calculations to determine the grade-level equivalent of a reading passage. These formulas are still useful and can be accessed through the Internet. Most computer word-processing programs will also give you a grade-equivalent score for any set of words you input.

But we know that mathematical calculations of sentences, words, and syllables are not enough to judge the reading difficulty of texts for children just learning to read.

PRINT FEATURES

The length of a book may not be technically related to its degree of difficulty; for example, some complex books are very short, and some very easy texts have many pages. However, a long book can be intimidating for young readers. Most emergent-level texts have 8 or 16 pages with only a few words on each page.

The appearance of print on the page also influences its accessibility to readers. At the earliest levels, both the size of type and spaces between words is large, with the print placed in the same location on every page. Short labels for pictures evolve into phrases, sentences, and paragraphs as the level of difficulty increases.

Another consideration is where the line breaks occur. Supportive texts for early readers break sentences into meaningful phrases; at higher levels, breaks occur simply to accommodate justification of type at the end of the line.

PREDICTABILITY AND ILLUSTRATIVE SUPPORT

Language patterns and text structures help make texts predictable. Our youngest readers rely on memory and pictures to access texts, so repeated phrases and sentences are necessary supports. Illustrations can carry the text or can simply enhance and extend the story line. Texts for independent readers are unlikely to have any patterns and often have no illustrations.

COMPLEXITY OF THEMES AND CONCEPTS

At the simplest reading levels, story lines are based on events and ideas that young readers are likely to have experienced directly. Imaginative stories with more complex plots and well-developed characters, such as Junie B. Jones or Franklin the Turtle, are more challenging for the reader. Folk tale and fantasy genres are usually not found in emergent- and early-level texts. Layers of meaning, multiple episodes, and events beyond the realm of experience of the reader require a much higher level of maturity on the part of the reader.

Reader response theory tells us that readers brings a unique set of experiences and background to what they read; therefore, each reader will have a different experience with a given text. The more mature the reader, the more likely a range of experiences and vocabulary will enable the reader to understand and appreciate a particular text. As well, the background experiences of a reader will influence the level of a text for that reader. For example, a child from the prairies may experience difficulty with even a simple text on ocean creatures.

LANGUAGE STRUCTURES

Words and sentences are important indicators of reading difficulty. Easier texts are dominated by high frequency and decodable words; more difficult texts contain descriptive vocabulary and literary language, such as figures of speech.

Sentence complexity is another readability factor. Texts for Guided Reading range from single words and phrases, to simple choppy sentences, to longer sentences with embedded clauses and rhythmical structures.

Leveling your School Book Collection

A full inventory will let you know where the strengths and gaps are in your leveled reading collection, so you can use resources wisely when you have opportunities to supplement the collection.

You want to establish a leveled book collection in your school, with an assortment of books scattered throughout various classrooms and the resource centre. Here's how to get started. Work with your colleagues to gather all the early-reading materials from individual classrooms to a common bookroom. You'll likely be surprised at the size of your collection when you put all the books together! The structure of Guided Reading is such that no one ever needs *all* the books at any one time; putting the resources together ensures that everyone will have access to the materials they need when they need them.

It will simplify the leveling process considerably if you use a commercial program or leveled book lists available from publishers. However, it's quite likely that you will eventually encounter a title that is not on the list—or you may disagree with a level that has been assigned to a book you know. Therefore you should familiarize yourself with what books look like at each level.

On the other hand, you may not have access to a published book list, or you may want to create your own leveling system. A simple way to organize your leveled book collection is to start by sorting your books onto four tables: Emergent, Early, Developing, and Fluent. The rubric on page 36 is a detailed description of books at each level according to key criteria, but here is a very simple guide:

- If the book has large print, lots of illustrations, and a heavy pattern that is repeated over and over, put it on the Emergent table.
- If the book has short sentences, a very simple story line, and mostly high-frequency and decodable words, put it on the Early table.
- If the book has several choppy sentences on a page, has smaller print, and appears to cover more complex concepts and characters, put it on the Developing table.
- If the book seems more difficult than the ones described above, and has literary language, put it on the Fluent table.

Now go back and look at the books on each table. You may decide to move some of them from one table to another. For example, a book that looked quite simple and short at first may have more difficult vocabulary than an early reader can cope with. A good rule of thumb is this: When in doubt, move a book to a higher level. It never hurts for a group of readers to work with a text that is easy for them.

You may want to sort the texts further. Take the books on each table and make three groups: easy, average, and hard. Now you have four major categories with three subgroups in each—a total of twelve levels that will address the needs of most of your readers in Grade 1 and 2, and perhaps even Grade 3.

Now that you have sorted the texts, you may want to code them in some way: colored sticky dots on the spine or cover may indicate specific levels. A simple system is to use a different color for each level, then use one dot for easy, two dots for average, and three dots for difficult at that level. In other words, a higher-level early text may be coded with three yellow dots on the cover.

Store the books in one or more large boxes or tubs labeled with the level. Text sets of four to six books should be stored together in a bag and set aside for Guided Reading. Individual titles may be kept in the appropriate tub and used for Browsing Boxes or independent reading practice.

CHALLENGES OF LEVELING FLUENT-LEVEL TEXT

Assessing readability becomes increasingly difficult as the texts become more complex. For one thing, there is a huge range of materials, from Dr. Seuss to the Bible. Judgments about reading levels are made more on the basis of complexity of concepts than size of print or predictability, which means that each student's background experience will have a different impact on the ability to understand and relate to the story.

Using a commercial readability formula or published book list is probably the best starting point for leveling more advanced texts. You will need to access your own professional knowledge to help you match these texts to the needs and interests of your students. A quick oral reading record and comprehension check can be used to guide your judgment.

MANAGING AND STORING YOUR LEVELED BOOK COLLECTIONS

Schools have found many creative ways to organize their leveled book collections. One easy way is to store each book set in its own resealable bag with a pocket and sign-out card on the outside. All the book bags at each level are stored in a labeled tub. When a teacher needs books for Guided Reading, he or she can simply go to the bookroom and sign out an appropriate level book bag for each student.

Usually, teachers like to keep a book set for three or four days after it has been used for a Guided Reading lesson, so the students can revisit the text for reading practice. After about four days, a book set can be cycled back into the bookroom.

Some places to store bookroom collections include an unoccupied classroom, a corner of the resource centre, or even a cupboard in the hallway. Regardless of the storage location, bookroom collections operate most efficiently when the whole class cooperates in signing out books, returning them promptly, and taking care of the books.

The Limits of Leveling

Leveled reading materials are intended for teaching purposes. They expedite the process of finding texts that are at the instructional reading levels of your students (see Chapter 4 Assessing Students for more on instructional and frustration reading levels). Instructional-level texts are intended to be read with support from the teacher.

Your students need exposure to a wide range of texts in their language arts program. They need instructional-level texts for strategy learning. They need exposure to more challenging texts in read-alouds and shared book experiences to extend higher-level thinking. And they need plenty of access to easy texts for independent reading practice. Your students should not be limited to instructional-level texts for independent reading, nor should they be required to read frustration-level texts on their own.

Characteristics of Texts at Each Reading Level

Level	*Print*	*Predictability*	*Concepts*	*Language*	*Example*
Emergent	• Large print, consistently placed on page • Large spaces between words • 8–16 pages • Single words, phrases, or sentences on each page	• Highly predictable • Word or sentence patterns • Illustrations provide direct support for text	• Familiar objects and actions • More labeling of pictures than story line • Experiences common to young readers	• Simple, familiar language • Mostly concept words—nouns and verbs • Increasing numbers of high-frequency words • May be words, phrases, or simple sentences	*Brown Bear, Brown Bear, What Do You See?* by Bill Martin, Jr.
Early	• Large print • More print on each page • 16–24 pages • few sentences on each page	• Some repetitive, cumulative, or chronological structures • Illustrations provide moderate support for text	• Simple story lines • Familiar events and experiences	• Mostly high-frequency and decodable words • New vocabulary frequently repeated • More sentences on each page • Line breaks at meaningful phrases	*Happy Birthday Moon* by Frank Asch
Developing	• Variation in print size and placement • Some unusual fonts • Up to 32 pages • Beginning of division into paragraphs	• Not predictable • Illustrations support the story line rather than the text	• Topics no longer relate directly to readers' experience • Beginnings of folk tales, fairy tales • May be several characters	• Two-part sentences with conjunctions and prepositions • Higher ratio of unique vocabulary to familiar and decodable words	*Frog and Toad* by Arnold Lobel
Fluent	• Conventional print size • Entire pages of text • Paragraphs and chapters	• Not predictable • May have no illustrations	• Complete range of themes and topics	• Complex sentences with embedded clauses • Descriptive and figurative language	*The Paper Bag Princess* by Robert Munsch

If your child reads with...	*...the text is considered to be at his or her...*	*...and should be used for...*
96–100% accuracy and thorough comprehension	independent reading level	lots of reading practice
90–95% accuracy and general comprehension	instructional reading level	teaching purposes
Below 90% accuracy and/or inadequate comprehension	frustration reading level	read-alouds or shared reading

Reading researcher Dick Allington (2000) suggests that 20% of the reading kids do in school should be at their instructional reading level, and the other 80% at their independent reading level. Plenty of easy reading is important for students to build fluency, practise strategies, and refine skills. Many teachers and parents have the misconception that children need challenging texts in order to practise their reading. The truth is that bulk reading of easy texts is what gives us practise and builds fluency.

It doesn't take a mathematical genius to figure out that this leaves no time for children to have to read frustration-level text. However, we all know of situations in which a child is so interested in a topic or so motivated to read a particular book that she or he will struggle through a text that is well beyond independent or instructional level. We can offer supports such as buddy reading or audiotapes, but we must remember that these activities do little to help the student develop independent reading strategies.

Ultimately, we want to help students gain skill in selecting their own books for independent reading. If we want them to be lifelong readers, they must learn to choose books that they will *want* and *be able* to read. One way to teach students to assess the difficulty of a book for themselves is to use the Five Finger Rule shown on page 19.

Sometimes parents are unsure of how to help their children with home reading. If you are allowing students to select their own books for home reading, they will sometimes bring home books they can read on their own, but at other times they will choose books that are too difficult for independent reading. Take-home reading bookmarks (see BLM page 39) are a good tool for guiding parents as they participate in reading with their students. Keep a collection of these bookmarks (color coded by copying them onto colored paper) on hand and, as students go out the door, tuck the appropriate bookmark into each student's home reading selection to guide parents in reading to their children, reading along with their children, or listening to their children read independently.

Choosing a Balance of Genres and Text Forms

Story books and novels have always dominated our reading programs in schools. We know that our students can learn much about life and learning from reading realistic fiction, multicultural folk tales, fantasy stories, and the like. But we must remember that non-fiction—newspapers, brochures, maps, reports—dominates much of the reading we do in life. We have a responsibility to build non-fiction texts into our Guided Reading program as well. (See Chapter 14 for a discussion of Using Non-fiction in the Guided Reading program).

Guided Reading lessons are, of necessity, short and purposeful. When we select texts to serve our learning objectives, we must be mindful of the limited time frame. With more sophisticated readers, a lengthy text may be used over a series of lessons, or students may be assigned to read portions independently between Guided Reading lessons. But don't forget the value of short texts for all readers. Novels and book-length info-texts are only part of the program. Short stories, magazine articles, excerpts, and selections from anthologies are just some of the shorter texts that can be used in Guided Reading for strategy instruction. Again, let's be sure to provide our students with some balance in the types of texts they study.

Choosing a suitable text is one of the keys to an effective Guided Reading lesson. While leveling formulas can be useful, successful leveling requires knowledge of the reading process, the books, and your students. No one can provide that combination but you.

It has been said that if a child doesn't like to read, it simply means we haven't found the right book for that child. Finding one right book for can set that child on the road to being a reader for life.

Take-Home Reading Bookmarks

Read *to* your child

- Sit together as you read.
- Talk about pictures and story together.
- Share your own reactions and favorite parts.
- Invite your child to comment as you read.

Read *by* your child

- Your child should be able to read this on his/her own.

- Sit with your child as s/he reads.
- Provide the word if s/he gets stuck.
- If the book seems to be too hard, read it to him/her.

Read *with* your child

- Have your child read the parts s/he can read and you fill in the rest.
- Take turns reading paragraphs or pages.
- Have your child join in on repeated phrases.
- Read parts together in unison.

4 Assessing Students and Creating Groups

In balanced literacy classrooms, students are grouped in different ways for different purposes throughout the day. Sometimes we allow students to select their own reading partners or bus buddies. Sometimes students who share a common interest are grouped for literature circles or a particular research project. Sometimes we place students in groups that have similar instructional needs. Guided Reading groups are formed with students who are at common levels of reading proficiency and need the same strategy instruction.

When students have many opportunities to work in different kinds of groups for different purposes, ability-based groups for Guided Reading are not an issue. But it is important to ensure that needs-based reading groups are only a small part of the school day; students should have many opportunities for different grouping structures as well as individual and whole-class instruction. It is also essential that reading groups are *flexible*. Assessments should be used frequently to ensure that students are placed appropriately and to move them when necessary.

This chart demonstrates some of the different grouping strategies used for different purposes in classrooms.

Assignment	*How*	*Purpose*	*Examples*
Random	Arbitrary	Management convenience	Table groups or reading partners
Interest	Grouped by common interest	To undertake a collaborative project	To research a topic of interest or prepare a joint project
Skill or need	Grouped by proficiency level or need for a particular skill	To teach that skill to students who need and are ready for it	Guided Reading groups

Assessment is the key to forming and maintaining Guided Reading groups. That means we must find out what our students know and can do as readers. This allows us to plan instruction that most effectively meets their needs and to place them with others who can benefit from the same instruction. Assessment does not mean we need to administer formal standardized tests; in fact, such tests do not always give us the information we need to guide classroom instruction. Quick and frequent classroom assessments that are integrated into the reading program will give us useful snapshots of both our students' reading progress and their instructional needs.

Oral Reading Records

The single most effective tool for assessing reading is the oral reading record. Like the traditional informal reading inventory, the oral reading record keeps track of behaviors and errors a student makes as he reads aloud. Noted New Zealand educator Marie Clay developed a coding system that teachers could use to take an the oral reading record on any piece of text, enabling teachers to conduct the assessment "on the run"; hence the term "running record" for one form of the oral reading record. Rather than requiring an extra copy of the text for marking the students' errors, Dr. Clay taught teachers to use a blank piece of paper on which to mark each word read correctly and record words read incorrectly.

Ken Goodman introduced the process of miscue analysis based on the premise that, when readers substitute words for those in the text, they are not making mistakes, but miscues; word substitution is evidence that they are simply not using their cueing systems effectively. Goodman says that miscues are "windows into the reading process" that can give a teacher a clear picture of which cueing systems a student knows how to use and which he or she needs to learn.

When combined with a miscue analysis and comprehension assessment, the oral reading record provides invaluable information for planning instruction to match the strengths and needs of your students. Teachers can also note reading behaviors such as self-monitoring, fluency and expression, repeated words and phrases, and hesitations. The Oral Reading Record Sheet on page 42 may be used to keep track of the information acquired in this assessment.

Oral reading records are intended to help teachers

- monitor ongoing student progress in reading
- find out particular skills and strategies students are using
- focus on specific needs of individual children
- group children with similar needs for reading instruction
- choose books at an appropriate level for students

Using Oral Reading Records to Group Students

At a level of 90-95% accuracy, text is considered to be at* instructional level *because it has the right balance of support and challenge: the reader can read most of the text with ease, yet must do some reading work in order to understand it completely.

An oral reading record provides an indication of how well a student can read a particular text. Not only does it help us see which students are at similar levels of proficiency, it also indicates what texts are most appropriate for teaching these students. Research indicates that when a child can read 90–95% of the words in a text, that text is at the optimal level of difficulty for teaching that student.

Oral reading records can be used with any text. However, when these records are being used to determine grouping and text selection for Guided Reading, it is best to use graded or leveled reading passages. If you have access to leveled book collections (see Chapter 3), use your professional judgment to select a book as a starting point. If the student reads the book with ease (that is, greater than 90% accuracy), go to a higher level (more difficult book), and continue in this way until you reach a text that the student reads with 90–95% accuracy. Similarly, if the student is obviously experiencing difficulty with the text, stop the reading and choose a lower level (easier) text. Text that a student reads with less than 90% accuracy is deemed to be at *frustration level*, for obvious reasons.

Oral Reading Record Sheet

TITLE:

Student's Name: *Date:*

Accuracy Check

Total Number of Words: ________
Number of Words Read Correctly: _____

Words Read Correctly x 100
Total Number of Words

= Percentage Accuracy: _________

$\frac{WRC}{TNW} \times 100 = PA$

Cueing Strategies
Percentage of miscues in which the student applied this strategy. Note that more than one strategy may be applied even when a miscue is made.

Meaning (Context): _______
Language Structure: ________
Visual (Phonics): _______

Dominant Cueing Strategy: ______________
Weakest Cueing Strategy: ________________

Fluency

❑ Fluent Reading ❑ Non-Fluent Reading ❑ Uses Punctuation

Retelling
Characters *yes* ....*no*

Plot *yes* ....*no*

Inference *yes* ....*no*

❑ Comprehensive Understanding
❑ General Understanding
❑ Needs help

Comprehension Questions

Literal Comprehension
1.
2.
3.
4.

Inferential Comprehension
1.
2.

❑ Comprehensive Understanding
❑ General Understanding
❑ Needs Help

If you do not have access to leveled books, or if your students are beyond Grade 2, start with a book that has been designated *grade level* for your grade. There are many sources for determining the level of a book. Sometimes the grade-level equivalent will be indicated right on the back of the book. A readability formula may be applied as a starting point. As well, there are increasing numbers of published lists of leveled books, including Fountas and Pinnell's *Matching Texts and Readers*.

Again, if the student can read a text with over 96% accuracy, his or her independent reading level, try again with a more difficult text; if it is at his or her frustration level, less than 90% accuracy, use an easier text.

Tip

Before the student reads, take a quick word count and figure out how many miscues he or she must make in order to reach instructional level. Then, you can stop the reading before the student hits frustration level in the reading.

A 100-word passage is adequate for conducting a running record, though you will probably want to allow the student to continue until he or she reaches a logical stopping point. A useful tip for teachers is to find the word count before reading, and calculate the number of miscues that would register as instructional reading level. Then you can quickly judge if the text is too difficult for a student. A general rule of thumb is that if you can't keep up with recording errors, then the text is probably too difficult for the student. There is no point in drawing out a frustrating reading experience.

Word-level accuracy is not always enough to determine instructional level; there are always some students who are able to decode with ease, but do not necessarily comprehend what they read. A comprehension assessment using questions or retelling helps provide necessary additional information about the student's strategic reading.

If a student can read a text with accuracy but without comprehension, that text is at frustration level. It is important to consider both accuracy and comprehension when determining instructional-level texts.

Accuracy	*Comprehension*	*Level*
96–100%	Comprehensive	Independent
96–100%	Weak	Instructional
90–95%	Comprehensive	Instructional
90–95%	General	Instructional
90–95%	Weak	Frustration
Below 90%	Comprehensive	Instructional
Below 90%	General	Frustration
Below 90%	Weak	Frustration

Remember that taking an oral reading assessment does not level a reader; rather, it tells you what types of texts are most suitable for teaching that reader. It also helps you make judgments about which readers will have similar needs and can be grouped together for instruction.

Conducting an Oral Reading Record

1. Select a passage of about 100 words (fewer for younger readers) for the student to read. Although many teachers prefer to conduct a running record on a blank sheet of paper, teachers who are just beginning to work with oral reading records will find it easiest to create a copy of the text on which to mark miscues.
2. Sit beside the student and explain that you want the student to read a book to you.
3. Read the title of the book to the student and give a one-sentence summary of the book that may include key names. For example, "This book is called *What a Story!* It is about a girl named Sara who has trouble writing stories for her teacher."
4. Give the child the book and use a record form with the text reproduced, or a blank sheet of paper, to mark reading behavior and record miscues.
5. When a student stops during reading, allow enough time for him or her to work out the problem before you provide help.
6. Record words that are read correctly, as well as substitutions, omissions, and deletions. You can develop your own coding system or use a standard system such as the one provided below.
7. Take note of self-corrections. When students correct their own miscues, it is an indication that they are monitoring their own comprehension.
8. You may also wish to note hesitations, repetitions, and other reading behaviors that may not affect accuracy but provide information about the strategies the reader is using.
9. If the student is blocked on a word, you may choose to intervene in order to move the reading along. This is a professional judgment, based on your knowledge of the student and the reading situation. Whenever possible, students should be required to make an attempt at every word. Be sure to note any information that is told by you.

Tip

Resist the temptation to teach the student as he or she reads! Remember that the purpose of this task is to assess what the students can do independently.

One of the biggest concerns for teachers just beginning to work with oral reading records is the amount of one-on-one time it requires. This is why it is a good idea to establish independent learning routines first, so that the other students are engaged in literacy activities while you pull out one student at a time. We also need to remind ourselves that, as instructional time, conducting assessments is as legitimate and valuable as standing in front of our students, chalk in hand.

RECORDING MISCUES

Recording reading miscues is a process that requires practice to gain speed and efficiency. As you become more proficient, you may want to develop your own coding systems to record various types of information about your students' reading.

A good starting point, however, is to record the following four types of miscues: substitutions, omissions, insertions, and self-corrections. "Teacher assists" should also be recorded as miscues, but it is a good idea to discourage students from appealing for words; instead, encourage them to use their decoding skills to make a try at every word.

Substitution – Write the substituted word or sounds above the correct word
Omission – Draw a circle around the omitted word in the text
Insertion – Use a caret to write in the inserted word
Self-correction – Note self-corrections with *SC* as well as a notation of what the attempts sounded like
Teacher Assist – If you choose to tell the student a word, mark it with a *T*

CALCULATING ACCURACY

- Substitutions, omissions, and insertions are counted as miscues.
- Names count as a miscue only once.
- Words other than names count as a miscue each time they are read incorrectly.
- Teacher-assisted words are counted as miscues.
- Self-corrections do *not* count as miscues.

Calculate accuracy percentage by dividing the number of words read correctly by the total number of words and multiplying by 100.

Calculate accuracy percentage by dividing the number of words read correctly by the total number of words and multiplying by 100.

MISCUE ANALYSIS

A miscue analysis is an evaluation of the causes of the miscues the student is making. For each miscue, try to determine whether the child is using cues from the meaning (semantics), the structure of the language (syntax), the visual information contained in the print (graphophonics), or a combination of these.

For self-corrections, you may also want to analyze what led the student to make this error and what cueing system was used to correct it, although you may not be able to identify discrete cues. A self-correction is often an indication that the reader is using cueing systems flexibly.

When analyzing miscues, ask yourself three questions:

- "Does it make sense?" If so, the reader has used meaning cues.
- "Does it sound grammatically correct?" If so, the reader has used syntax.
- "Does it match the print?" If so, the reader has used graphophonics.

Say, for example, a reader makes the following miscue:

sparks
When I turned on the computer, ~~smoke~~ came out.

This reader has used meaning (the miscue makes sense), syntax (the sentence structure is correct) and, to some degree, graphophonics (the beginning sounds are the same).

In the following miscue, the story makes sense and sounds right, but the miscue does not match the print; in other words, the reader did not use visual (graphophonic) cues:

nothing
When I turned on the computer, ~~smoke~~ came out.

Students who have learned to decode may make miscues similar to the following:

smoking
When I turned on the computer, ~~smoke~~ came out.

In this case, the reader has relied almost exclusively on graphophonics. The miscue does not make sense, nor is it syntactically acceptable.

Miscue analysis requires us to read the mind of the reader. Sometimes it will be difficult to tell whether a reader has applied a particular cueing system. At other times, a reader may use all cueing systems, but still make a miscue. All of this is valuable information for the teacher. The aim of reading instruction is for the child to use cue sources in a flexible and integrated manner in order to word solve accurately and efficiently, and to comprehend adequately.

Checking on Comprehension

There are two main ways teachers assess comprehension from an oral reading record: comprehension questions and retelling.

Comprehension questions are a fairly simple strategy. If you use comprehension questions, be sure to ask a combination of literal and inferential questions, in order to get the big picture of the student's comprehension. For example, a question like "What came out of the computer when she turned it on?" is literal information because the answer comes directly from the text. A question like "Why do you think smoke came out of the computer?" requires the reader to make inferences from the text.

One disadvantage of comprehension questions is that sometimes students can respond correctly to the questions without truly understanding the text. Furthermore, asking questions focuses the reader's thinking in particular directions.

Retelling, on the other hand, is an opportunity for the reader to recount those parts of the story he or she remembers and finds important. It does not box in the reader's thinking. Instead, it tells you what the child knows about story structure, vocabulary, sequencing, and the relative importance of information, as well as details from the story.

If you use retelling as an assessment strategy, it is important to teach the students what you expect. Retelling is also a good comprehension tool for the reader. It helps students synthesize the reading and focus on the salient elements of the story.

Before students read, tell them, "When you have finished reading/listening to this book, I would like you to tell me about it in your own words." After reading, say, "Pretend that I've never heard this story and tell me everything about it," or "Pretend you are telling this story to a friend who has never heard it." If a student is having difficulty getting started, prompt with, "This story is about..." If a student stops before giving all information, encourage her or him to continue by asking questions like "What comes next?" or "What else do you remember?"

Tip

Comprehension assessments are generally unnecessary for emergent-level texts. Often there is not enough information to retell in these beginning books. Also, because emergent readers rely on memory and pictures to read, we can assume that if they say the words accurately, they are likely to be comprehending adequately.

Retellings may be oral or written, but an oral retelling is often most expedient, especially for young children. It enables the reader to focus on the story rather than the writing, and enables the teacher to note the retelling process and provide prompting as necessary.

The retelling can give you useful information about what your students understand, remember, and consider important about the story. The Retelling Record Sheet on page 130 is a helpful tool for assessing each student's retelling. More information on how to teach retelling may be found in Chapter 13.

Practical Considerations

Conducting oral reading records is time-consuming, but it is well worth the time. An oral reading record provides us with valuable information about a child's reading proficiency and habits. We need to remind ourselves that assessment is an important part of teaching. How else do we determine what our students already know and what they need to learn?

Take the time to establish the independent learning routines that will underlie your Guided Reading program. For the first few weeks, instead of working with reading groups, conduct oral reading records while the students are engaged in independent learning activities. After the initial assessments, you will need to conduct the oral reading records less frequently, depending on the reading levels of the students and the progress they are making. Some teachers like to begin each Guided Reading lesson with a quick oral reading assessment of one student, while other teachers conduct oral reading records as needs warrant. When it seems to the teacher that one or more students are ready to move on to a higher level of texts, a quick oral reading record can confirm that judgment.

Some people prefer to send their students to a quiet place to audiotape their own reading. Then the teacher can listen to the tape and record miscues at another time. The advantages of this system are that the teacher is not tied up while the student is reading, and that the teacher can listen to the tape at his or her convenience, rewinding and repeating the tape to keep up with the recording. On the other hand, a teacher can learn much from observing a student's behavior while reading. As well, if the student gets bogged down in the reading, it is impossible to adjust the text or provide the necessary support if the teacher is not observing directly.

Assessment is an essential element of the Guided Reading program. Give it the necessary time and attention, and you will find it a vital component of instruction.

Creating and Maintaining Guided Reading Groups

Calculating the instructional reading level of your students will tell you what kinds of texts will be most appropriate for each student. You can then form groups with students who are at similar levels of development.

The number of groups in your classroom will depend on the students, their reading abilities, and your own teaching style. For most teachers, four groups are quite manageable. Research suggests that there should be about four to eight students in a group. Students who need more reading support should be in smaller groups. The more independent your students, the more capable they are of functioning in larger groups. However, it must be remembered that the larger the group, the less opportunity each student will have to participate. If you have a large number of students at about the same level, they might be split into two Guided Reading groups. The number of groups will depend on the diversity of students and management issues in the classroom.

If you are just getting started with Guided Reading, you may want to start with a couple of high-needs groups and retain your existing structure with the other students. As you and your students become more comfortable with the Guided Reading and independent work routines, you can add more GR groups or split up some of your larger groups.

Remember that the initial reading assessment is just a starting point. Your own professional judgment, anecdotal records and checklists, and frequent oral reading records assessments will enable you to maintain Guided Reading instruction that scaffolds your students to increasingly higher levels of development.

Your oral reading records will give you an indication of the kinds of books that are most appropriate for each of your reading groups. You will be able to group the students who are reading at the same levels, and use texts from your leveled book collection to plan Guided Reading instruction. It is important to remember that Guided Reading groups are flexible; we need to move students to higher levels of texts as needed. Frequent oral reading records help us assess each student's needs and plan grouping, texts, and strategic instruction to take every one of them to the next level of proficiency.

5 Principles of Guided Reading Instruction

What does the Guided Reading lesson look like? How can we take best advantage of the short time frame to help our students become strategic readers?

Planning the Guided Reading Lesson

Start with a Strategy

Good teaching begins with the end in mind. The first step in planning Guided Reading is deciding what you want the students in the group to learn. Our goal in Guided Reading instruction is to help our students develop the strategies they need in order to become independent, lifelong readers. These strategies may range from self-questioning, to making personal connections, to word-solving. Time is too valuable to spend on low-level comprehension questions that do nothing to build strategic independence. In planning the Guided Reading lesson, ask yourself *first* what your students are learning about becoming better readers, and *second* what your students are learning about a specific piece of text.

Focus on one strategy at a time, and spend time practising that strategy over several lessons. Research tells us that a strategy will have to be reinforced up to seven times before it becomes automatic! **(First Steps, 1994)**

No publisher can tell you what your students know and can do, and what they need to learn next. Your ongoing assessments, your relationships with your students, and your professional knowledge of the reading process are the best sources of information for determining learning objectives for your Guided Reading lessons.

Carefully Choose Materials

We have already discussed leveled reading materials at length in Chapter 3. It's critical to note that, particularly as our students become more mature, their background experiences and vocabulary base have a huge impact on the degree of difficulty of a particular text for a particular student. Determining reading levels includes considering the familiarity of concepts and language levels for your students.

You also want to make sure that the text provides opportunities for teaching the objectives you have set out. If you want to work on making inferences, for example, you must ensure that the text you select has different layers of meaning. If you are concerned about your students' knowledge of a particular language concept, such as adding *-ed* to words, look for texts with many examples of that concept.

Another text consideration is balancing genres and forms of writing. In reading instruction, we have tended to over-rely on fictional stories. But it is every bit as important for our students to develop strategies for reading various forms of non-fiction, as well as poetry. For a discussion of using non-fiction texts in the Guided Reading program, see Chapter 14.

Before Reading, During Reading, and After Reading

There are three main steps in planning Guided Reading instruction:

1. ***Determine your learning objectives.***
2. ***Choose appropriate reading materials that match the instructional level of the group.***
3. ***Plan for before-reading, during-reading, and after-reading components.***

Ensure that every lesson includes before-reading, during-reading, and after-reading components. Traditional reading instruction has often devoted more time and attention to after-reading activities than to the reading itself. Yet before-reading activities lay an important foundation for the reading. And, in truth, the real reading work is done *while* we read! We need to teach students to attend to strategy use during reading. Balanced attention to all three stages of the reading lesson helps students understand and take advantage of the whole reading process.

What a Guided Reading Lesson Looks Like

The Guided Reading lesson generally lasts 20 to 30 minutes. During this time, the teacher introduces a new book, supports the students as they read it independently, then extends the reading to build strategic independence and higher-level thinking.

Just as you establish routines for those working independently, you want to establish routines for the Guided Reading lesson, in order to maximize the use of instructional time and minimize time lost to transitions. One routine many teachers use is to start the lesson with reading practice of familiar texts.

After you finish each Guided Reading lesson, give the students their own copy of the book to reread for practice. This will provide each student with a collection of four or five little books from previous lessons. A small box is just right for holding three or four books. Each student's name is printed on the side of the box. Before coming to the Guided Reading lesson, each student picks up his or her box of books and simply reads these books until the teacher is ready for the lesson. At the end of the lesson, all the students return the oldest book to the classroom collection and add that day's book to their book boxes.

Use the small boxes that snacks come in, labeled with each student's name, for individual collections of familiar books.

This routine eases the transition to Guided Reading, and keeps the students in the group productively engaged in reading practice. It also frees up the teacher for a few minutes to take running records, get materials ready, or see to issues that may have come up with the rest of the students in the class.

READING PARTNERS

Because you are working with small groups of students, it will be possible to monitor each student's participation and ensure that every child has an opportunity to share ideas. Even within small groups, however, it will be advantageous to create reading partners for various purposes. Students may be invited to share predictions, connections, questions, and responses with their partner. An effective technique is to invite students to tell the group what their *partner* said. This encourages both active listening and efficient communication. Another time, you might ask reading partners to discuss the answer to a question and come up with a common solution. In this way, each student has more opportunity to think and share than he or she would in a group.

Some teachers prefer the structure of semi-permanent partners. In these cases, students work with the same reading partner as long as both remain in the group. In other Guided Reading groups, partnerships are formed casually by inviting students to "turn to the person beside you."

Reading partners within the Guided Reading groups can

- discuss personal connections, predictions, and reactions
- report the partner's ideas to the group
- come up with common answers to questions
- work together on assigned reading tasks

Students do not always need to be guided in their discussion. You can occasionally tell your students to "say something" about the book to their partners. They simply turn to their partners and make whatever observation comes to mind. In this way, students learn to make independent responses and apply the tools that have been provided for them.

Tip

As a signal for reading partners tell students, "Face to face and knee to knee, turn to your partner, 1-2-3."

Before Reading

The Book Introduction

The book introduction may well be the most critical aspect of the Guided Reading lesson. It enables the teacher to provide the delicate scaffolding that supports the students in reading most of the text, but also to leave something for students to work on themselves.

Some teachers like to distribute individual copies of the book for students to follow during the book introduction. Others feel that, by holding up the book themselves, they are better able to focus the students' attention on specific elements. It's a personal choice that may vary according to the students, the text, and the learning situation.

The book introduction enables the teacher to access prior knowledge, to highlight key language structures, to introduce concepts, or to set purposes for reading. The extent of the book introduction will vary according to the needs and developmental levels of the students, but will include some or all of the following on the part of the teacher.

Components of the book introduction and preview include

- ***Presenting the title, author, and publication information***
- ***Giving a summary statement***
- ***Guiding students to make connections***
- ***Setting purposes for reading***
- ***Inviting predictions***
- ***Previewing the book to introduce new vocabulary and concepts***

COVER AND PUBLICATION INFORMATION

The teacher presents the book title, author's name, illustrator's name, and other publication and cover information. For emergent-level readers, the title is likely to be the most difficult part of the text, and often presents key vocabulary essential to the story. Sometimes the "book's birthday" will be an interesting feature to the students, especially when the book is older than the students are!

SUMMARY STATEMENT

A one- or two-sentence overview of the book sets a context for making connections and predictions, accessing prior knowledge, and introducing key vocabulary.

GUIDE STUDENTS TO MAKE CONNECTIONS

We all learn new information best when we can connect it to information that we already know. In preparation for reading, invite students to make connections to their own experiences, previous reading, or knowledge about big issues in the world, such as friendship, racism, or caring for the environment. For more information on making text-to-self, text-to-text, and text-to-world connections, see Chapter 12 on Comprehension Strategies in the Guided Reading program.

SET A PURPOSE FOR READING

As independent readers, we know that we read differently for different purposes. Teaching students to think about their purpose for reading helps them to develop flexibility in their reading style and rate, and to set a context for reading.

With beginning readers, "I wonder…" statements help them focus on a particular aspect of the text. We might ask, "I wonder how Charlotte is going to help Wilbur" or "I wonder what animals we will find in this book on the zoo."

The purpose for reading may also address strategy use, such as, "I'd like you to read this section of the book and tell me what connections you might make to other books you have read."

INVITE PREDICTIONS

Predicting is another way to set a purpose for reading. Students may respond to the "I wonder…" statement with their own predictions. It is important not to abandon the predictions once they are made, but to revisit them during and after reading. Students need to learn that good readers constantly confirm or change their predictions as they read, based on the new information that they encounter.

PREVIEW THE BOOK

The picture walk, or pic-flic, is a technique used by many teachers to introduce a text for Guided Reading. The teacher guides the students through the text to make predictions, introduce unfamiliar concepts, and note unique vocabulary and language structures. At emergent levels, the teacher generally walks through every page to ensure that the students are introduced to all key words and patterns in context. At higher levels, the teacher may choose to walk through only selected pages, or none at all. The degree of support will vary with the needs of the students and the particular text they are reading.

Connie Watson is introducing a group of early readers to a new story. She knows these students will have little difficulty with most of the vocabulary, so her picture walk consists of only two or three pages. One of these pages contains this text: "Dad was cross." Opening the book to that page, she asks the students to look at the illustration to guess how Dad feels. They respond with words like "mad" and "angry." She spends a few minutes helping them generate other words that mean the same as "angry" before telling them that sometimes the word "cross" is used to mean "angry" or "annoyed." She then invites the students to find the word "cross" on the page, and to tell how they know that word is "cross" and not "mad" or "angry," thereby making the graphophonic as well as contextual connection.

Other Materials

One of the greatest advantages of the Guided Reading strategy is the simplicity of materials. Generally speaking, the book is the only tool you need! However, I like to keep a basket of materials handy for those teachable moments—a small magnetic whiteboard with markers and magnetic letters, scissors, highlighting tape, and other tools I may need for the lesson.

At upper levels, students will need access to writing tools for the Guided Reading lesson. Provide each student with a clipboard and attached pencil. Graphic organizers or blank paper can be distributed as needed for the lesson. Sticky notes and tabs are also important reading tools.

Tip

A trip to the discount or dollar store can yield a wonderful array of Guided Reading aids, such as magnetic letters and metal stove burner covers, "magic wands" for tracking, even "reading glasses" for finding special words.

During Reading

Tip

A Guided Reading toolkit for upper-level readers can be as simple as a laminated file folder cut into 10-cm strips. Attach three or four sticky notes in several different sizes for students to use in underlining words or ideas, marking points of confusion, or even writing questions or connections. The sticky notes may be reused and replaced as needed.

"Scaffolded reading is the heart of the Guided Reading lesson. It is here that students practice their growing array of skills and strategies and increase their fluency. It is here that teachers support and coach students individually." (Paulson and Nos, 2001)

Individual Reading

The during-reading phase of the Guided Reading lesson involves individual, independent reading of the text by the students. Remember that this is not round-robin reading. Students are not taking turns reading aloud, but are reading their own copies of the book, to themselves, at their own pace. During this scaffolded reading stage, the teacher circulates among the students, listening to them as they read. In this way, the teacher can make observations about strategy use, provide support on the spot, and make notes for planning future instruction. This provision of expert support to each individual at the moment of need may well be the greatest strength of the Guided Reading approach.

After introducing the book, distribute a copy of the text to each student and ask the students to read the book independently. You may want to read the first page together to provide additional support for emergent readers.

DISCOURAGING LOUD AND UNISON READING

Younger students will read aloud, sometimes very loudly! This is because beginning readers need the auditory feedback in order to know what they are reading. It will be necessary to teach them to read in quiet voices. Still, the problem of unison reading may occur. One way to prevent this is by providing students with elbows of PVC pipe to use as "reading phones." When a reader holds one end to his mouth and the other to his ear, the sound is magnified so that he can hear himself reading without disturbing others.

Tip

Although reading phones may be purchased commercially, they can be made simply and inexpensively from elbows of PVC pipe from the home improvement store.

Another solution to the problem of unison reading is to stagger the times when students in the Guided Reading group start to read.

> Reading specialist Becky Olness stagger starts the reading by saying, "Kyla and Jennifer, you may start reading, while the rest of you find your favorite picture in the book." Once Kyla and Jennifer have read about a page, she'll say, "Now Haley and Adam may start reading while the rest of you tell your reading buddies why you picked that picture as your favorite." She continues starting the students two at a time until all students have begun to read. Stagger starts mean that students finish at different times. Establish routines for what to do next. Encourage students to reread the text as many times as they can before the time is up. In this way, they are getting bulk reading practice and remain engaged in reading.

The Teacher's Role During Reading

While the students are reading, it is your role to listen to the students, in order to note strategy use and take advantage of teaching opportunities. Feel free to ask individual students to reread certain lines or passages to you. You will be able to anticipate most of the difficulties your students might experience, but some might surprise you. Grade 1 teacher Dawn Kesslering was amazed to find that one student in her emergent-level group was actually reading the book back to front! Provide assistance to students who need it and make plans for further instruction.

When a student makes a miscue, be sure to allow enough time for the student to self-correct before intervening. A wait time of about 3 to 5 seconds encourages the student to think for her- or himself, without interrupting the reading too long.

By the time students reach developmental and fluent levels, they should be reading silently. Since the teacher can no longer hear miscues the students are making, the teacher's role changes. You may ask students to read certain passages aloud. More often, you might assign students to read short sections of text for strategy practice.

After Reading

Traditionally, the after-reading component of the reading lesson was the one to which we devoted the most time and attention. But it may well be the *least* important part of the lesson. And, quite frankly, many of the things we've done in the interests of follow-up to reading—such as low-level comprehension questions or having students draw a picture—have contributed little to our students' growth as readers, writers, and thinkers.

After reading is the time to review and reinforce reading strategies. Acknowledge students who were using reading strategies. You may want to offer mini lessons on comprehension strategies or word study. Remember that mini lessons are, as the name implies, brief and focused. Choose only one concept or strategy to model and practise with the students.

Tip

Not every reading requires an extension activity. Often the best follow-up to reading is simply more reading!

Guided discussion is a key element of the Guided Reading lesson's after-reading component. Carefully structured questioning promotes higher-level thinking and extends experience with the text. A variety of written responses may be appropriate for students at higher reading levels. These may range from graphic organizers to response journals, depending on the needs and abilities of the students. Sometimes, the text may lend itself to an educationally sound extension or follow-up activity, such as role drama, readers theatre, visual art, or further research. Remember that any after-reading activities we undertake must help our students become better readers, writers, and thinkers.

Tailoring the Guided Reading Lesson

A well-planned Guided Reading lesson can both engage your students in a wonderful reading experience and build the skills and strategies for increasing independence. Our goal for Guided Reading is not just to ensure that our students learn something about a particular text, but to ensure that our students learn something about being a reader. Ultimately, we want to scaffold them through a reading experience in such a way that they will be able to tackle a similar experience on their own in the future. This means that the lesson structure will vary according to the strengths and needs of the students. The Guided Reading lesson will look somewhat different for students at the emergent, early, developmental, and fluent reading levels. The following chapters examine Guided Reading at each stage of reading proficiency.

A Guided Reading Lesson Plan

Title, Author and Publication Info: ______________________________

Level: ______________________ *Genre:* ______________________

Lesson Objectives (Strategy focus):

-
-

Before Reading

Connections:

Summary statement:

Preview:

I wonder…

Discussion Points

-
-
-

Creative Response or Extension:

	Language Feature	*Teaching Method*
High-frequency words		
Letter/Sound concepts		
Structural features (word)		
Text features		

6 Guided Reading for Emergent Readers

Jason is in Grade 1. He loves to spend time in the reading corner and can often be heard making up stories as he flips through the pages. In fact, he likes to invite the teacher and other students to listen to him "read." Jason sees himself as a reader and is unaware of the fact that he is not doing what we might consider real reading.

Kayla, also in Grade 1, loves to listen to stories. She can print her name and most of the alphabet letters. She knows that there is a "real" way to read and prefers to take out books that have been read in class so she can imitate the words and phrases she remembers.

Both Jason and Kayla are emergent readers. They are on the road to literacy, though what they do might not be considered reading by a layperson. Actually, they know a lot more about reading than may be evident to the untrained eye. They know that books tell a story. They know that books are read from front to back, and other concepts about print. They know the difference between pictures and writing, can identify many alphabet letters, and may even know some words, especially their own names. Most importantly, they want to learn to read and are quite confident that they can and will!

Emergent readers

- have mastered some concepts about print
- can listen to and tell a story
- know that print tells a story
- know the difference between pictures and print
- know some letters and sounds
- have a sense of story
- rely on pictures and memory when they "read"
- want to read and believe they can

The Guided Reading Lesson for Emergent Readers

Emergent readers have just begun the journey toward literacy. Because they have established few independent reading strategies, they need a great deal of teacher support. At this level, group size should be relatively small: groups of two to four students are probably optimal. The Guided Reading group should meet frequently, every day if possible, though the lessons do not need to be long. A 15- to 20-minute lesson is usually adequate. It is important to conduct frequent oral reading records, as many students progress quickly through this stage.

Some teachers believe that students who do not have a repertoire of high-frequency words or an understanding of letter–sound relationships are not yet ready for Guided Reading. Others feel that these students, more than any, benefit from a small group setting, using early emergent-level texts to focus instruction on their particular needs. Rather than having the students read independently, teachers may sometimes choose to use a shared reading approach to scaffold the students through the text. In this approach, they read the text in unison with the students before expecting students to read it on their own.

Areas of focus for emergent readers include the following:

- continuing development of oral language skills
- developing a repertoire of high-frequency words
- letters and their sounds, particularly consonants
- using beginning and ending sounds for decoding
- the concept of "word"
- using picture cues
- building confidence

As we work with emergent readers, we want them to continue to build their repertoire of high-frequency words. We want them to solidify their knowledge of letter–sound relationships so they can use graphophonics as a cueing strategy. Most children are able to hear the initial sounds in words first, then the final sounds. Medial vowels, especially short vowel sounds, are the most difficult to hear. This is why we start by asking readers to "get your mouth ready to say the word." When they pronounce the initial sound, it often helps them to decode the rest of the word. Later, we ask the students to "look across the word"; in other words, to attend to the rest of the letters.

One of the most important reading strategies for emergent readers is an understanding of the concept of "word," which is complex for young readers. When we speak, we don't hear separate words; we hear streams of words. But the understanding that words are separate entities "with space around them" is important for accessing written text. Voice-print matching, that is, saying a single word for each written word, is an essential strategy for readers.

Appropriate Texts for Emergent Readers

Emergent readers rely on memory and pictures to read. Therefore, texts for emergent readers should be very predictable, contain repeated patterns, and have strong support from pictures. In fact, many texts for emergent readers consist of little more than the labeling of pictures in words, phrases, or sentences. Language patterns that change only one or two concept words are appropriate at this stage, such as "This is a book. This is a desk." or "Fish swim in the water. Birds fly in the sky." The vocabulary in emergent-level texts consists mostly of high-frequency words and concept words, such as names of familiar objects, colors, and numbers.

Readers at this age are egocentric; they want to read about events and experiences they can relate to, such as a birthday party or a trip to the park.

Texts for emergent readers

- are predictable and heavily patterned
- contain limited amounts of text—a few words to one or two sentences
- place text in the same place on each page
- have illustrations that heavily support the text
- are usually based on a single, familiar concept
- repeat basic sight word vocabulary
- have only one or two word changes per page

- contain large print with large space between words and lines
- have little or no story line; often just labeling of pictures
- use concept words—one or two new words per page
- may change the pattern on the last page
- may have a title that is the most difficult reading in the text

Here is a typical example of an emergent-level text:

I can put on my T-shirt. I can put on my sunglasses.

Sun Fun by Elle Ruth Orav, illustrated by Lam Quach; Curriculum Plus, 2001. Reprinted with permission.

What the Lesson Looks Like

Emergent readers require more scaffolding of text than any other group. At first, the lesson may look more like a shared reading session, as the teacher guides the students through the entire book. Later, the students may take on increasing responsibility for reading the text independently.

BEFORE READING: BOOK INTRODUCTION

Remember that emergent readers, who are not yet able to decode, will not be able to read words that are not already in their speaking vocabularies.

The book introduction should be very thorough for emergent readers. In fact, it will probably be necessary to walk through the entire book to ensure that there are no words or concepts that are unfamiliar to the students.

> I was guiding a group of Grade 1 students through the reading of a simple alphabet book. When we came to "glove," the picture representing the letter *g*, the students said, "Mitt." I reminded them to listen for the "front-door sound" and to "get their mouths ready" by saying the *g* sound. "G-, G-, G-," the students repeated faithfully; then "G-mitt!" It was a strong reminder that no matter how many graphophonic supports we put in place for emergent readers, they must have the basic vocabulary to understand what they read. Start by introducing students to the features of the cover: the title, author, and illustrator. Provide a one- or two-sentence summary to set a context for the book.

Guide your students to make personal connections with the topic. "Have you ever been to a birthday party?" "Tell about a time when you helped make a pizza for supper." At this stage, most connections will be related to children's direct personal experiences, though it may be possible for your students to connect to other stories they have read or heard. You might ask, "Does this cover or title remind you of another story we've read?"

Close the discussion with an "I wonder..." statement to set a purpose for reading, such as "I wonder what kind of pizza they will make."

The picture walk, or pic-flic, is a technique in which the teacher guides the students through the text to make predictions, introduce unfamiliar concepts, and note unique vocabulary and language structures.

The picture walk, or pic-flic, is the most effective preview at this stage. Walk through the book, page by page, discussing the pictures and ensuring that students are exposed to any words and patterns they are likely to encounter. You may choose to point them out in the text; more often, you will simply draw students' attention to the words orally. I recommend that you hold the book yourself and not distribute copies to the students until it it's time for them to read independently. Some teachers even prefer to cover the print on the page so that students focus on the pictures and the oral language structures, and not on the letters on the page.

> One of my favorite texts for emergent readers is based on building compound words, such as "a sail, a boat, a sailboat." One page shows a "handbag," which most of my students identified as a "purse" during the pic-flic. It was a cue to me to talk about different names for a purse, and to focus on the language structure of "hand" and "bag." At this stage, the picture walk will likely take more time than the actual reading! But it is important to establish the words, patterns, and ideas that the students will have to negotiate when they read the text independently. Because repeated patterns are integral to emergent-level reading, students should be introduced to any patterns that may be in the text.

You may also want to model tracking, or pointing to each word as it is read. Show students where to start reading on the page and how to take a return sweep at the end of the line. Most emergent-level readers do not understand voice-print matching, or saying one word for each word on the page. Tracking helps them learn to attend to each word individually.

DURING READING: SCAFFOLDED READING

Distribute copies of the book so each student has his or her own copy to read independently. Because students at this stage will still be reading aloud, you may need to model using quiet voices as they read. Distribute reading phones or stagger start the reading to avoid all students reading in unison (see page 52). While waiting to begin reading, the students can be looking for words they know or pictures they like. They might tell their reading partners about their predictions or connections. Find ways to engage students in the text until it is their turn to read. Tell students that if they finish reading, they should read the book over and over until everyone is done. "See how many times you can read through the whole book before I tell you to stop!" This bulk reading helps the emergent reader develop good reading habits.

Tip

Give the students tracking tools, such as fake fingers, to encourage them to point out each word as they read.

As the students read, circulate among them, noting strategies and providing help as needed. At this stage, students will be using patterns, context, and pictures to negotiate the text. Encourage students to begin to apply letter–sound relationships as well as picture cues to solve unfamiliar words. Emergent readers should begin to use initial sounds in words; ending sounds will follow. Some prompts you might provide during reading include

- "Does the picture give you a clue?"
- "Get your mouth ready to say the word."

- "Remember the pattern you read on the last page?"
- "What's the front-door sound in that word?"
- "Look across the word."
- "Go back and try that word again."

Kayla was reading an emergent-level text about compound words. She correctly read the words "cup" and "cake," but instead of "cupcake" she looked at the picture and read "muffin." I drew her attention to the front-door sound of muffin—*m*—and asked Kayla what letter would be at the beginning of muffin. Then I pointed to the letter at the beginning of "cupcake" and noted that it was the same sound as the one that started "Corey," which was on our classroom name wall. With that scaffolding, as well as a reminder to look at the picture, Kayla was able to word-solve "cupcake."

AFTER READING

Emergent-level books are only 8 to 16 pages long, so often there isn't a lot of potential for follow-up. At this stage, reading practice is the best follow-up. Make sure that the students have the opportunity to read the book several times during the lesson and over subsequent days.

Tip

Put a sticky note on the back of the book for students to keep a tally of how often they read the book.

As children read, you will have plenty of opportunity to note strategies the students are using and those they need to work on. Be sure to praise students for using effective strategies: "Kayla, would you tell the others how you figured out that word 'cupcake'?" or "Nassi, what a good strategy you used when you went back and read that sentence over again." Use your observations to plan short, focused lessons for the whole group.

Some mini lessons you may choose to teach include

- strategy use
- concepts about print
- letters and sounds
- beginning and ending sounds
- high-frequency words
- the concept of "word"

PATTERN BOOKS

One way to provide extra reading practice is to help students create their own books based on the language patterns in their Guided Reading texts.

You can start by building the text as a modeled writing lesson or a shared writing activity, soliciting ideas from the students to put into the books. For example, if you have read a book about compound words, you may generate a list of other compound words. Each student chooses one word to print and illustrate in the same format as the book, then the pages are compiled into a class book.

Or each student may create his or her own little book by folding a page into four squares. It might be made from a copy, with some or all of the text provided: "Dear Santa, thank you for the _____." Or you might provide cut-up sentences for students to assemble onto the page and illustrate.

Here are some other ideas for take-home books:

- Texts of familiar songs or nursery rhymes, such as "Twinkle, Twinkle Little Star" or "Old McDonald Had a Farm"
- Concept books, such as those on colors, numbers, "things I bring to school," or "things we eat"

- Counting or alphabet books
- Stems such as "I can . . ." or "Here is a . . ."

Encourage students to read their books to as many people as possible. Include a page at the end of the book for parents and friends to sign their names if the book has been read to them.

Teaching Emphases to Use with Emergent Readers

Developing the Concept of "Word"

Tip

Discount or dollar stores carry many items that may be used for word framing or tracking:
- ***magnifying glasses***
- ***bubble wands***
- ***back scratchers***
- ***"witch fingers"***

One of the most challenging concepts about print for emergent readers is the understanding that speech is made up of individual words. One way to reinforce the concept that "words have spaces around them" is to get students to frame words, rather than just pointing to them. Have the students create finger frames with their thumbs and forefingers and frame specific words in the text. Some teachers tell their students to "hug" a word. Word framers help students isolate individual words on the page. They can purchased, or easily and inexpensively made from paper.

When students read around the room, they track every word displayed on the walls, using pointers, chopsticks, and even back scratchers. Many teachers have creative collections of tracking tools, including small toy sharks on a sticks that "munch" the words. Scrounge stores at Halloween for tools like "witch fingers" that the students can place over their own fingers for tracking.

> Sharlene Kujat, a Kindergarten teacher, teaches students about the concept of "word" by focusing, not on the words, but on the spaces between the words! Her students put their fingers on the spaces before and after words, and chant, "Space to space, there's a word."

High-frequency Words

It is important to make sure that emergent readers develop a repertoire of high-frequency words that they can identify automatically and write correctly. As young Tommy pointed out when he first began to read, "Ever since I learned that word 'the,' I see it in everything I read!"

Like any other language concepts, high-frequency words are best taught in the context of connected text. Most of the words in emergent-level text are high-frequency words and concept words. These words—which Marie Clay calls "anchor words"—should be presented during the book introduction and revisited after reading. Students might be asked to frame a specific word on a page, or to match words in the book to word cards. Pattern books that are created after reading should reinforce these high-frequency words, with increasing expectation that the students write the words themselves.

It's important that high-frequency words are taught a few at a time and reinforced regularly. Draw attention to the language features—how many letters, how many syllables, letter patterns. If there are words that look similar, like "went" and "want," teach them at separate times, and draw attention to their similarities and differences. Work with the children to develop strategies for telling them apart. Make sure you use a variety of learning modes to reinforce the words: say them, cheer them, shout them, sing them, print them on paper and in the air, and use plenty of actions. It is important for students to overlearn them so that these words are read automatically. For more information on teaching high-frequency words, see Chapter 11.

Concepts about Print

There are certain basic understandings that emergent readers must develop in order to lay the foundations for independent reading. They need concepts about print, such as reading left to right and top to bottom. They need phonological awareness, or the understanding that words are made up of sounds. They need knowledge of the alphabet letters and sounds. It is not possible to use an oral reading record with students who are not yet reading conventionally; however, the assessment on pages 62–63 may be used to evaluate students, guide instruction, and monitor progress. (For more on blending and segmenting onsets and rimes, see Chapter 10.)

ADMINISTERING THE TEST

Use an emergent-level text to conduct this assessment. Hand the closed book to the student *upside down* and *back cover facing the student.*
Ask/tell the student the following:

1. Can you show me the front cover?
2. Turn to the first page.
3. Can you show me where the words (or writing or printing) are?
4. Where would you go next?
5. Point to the words as I read them.

LETTER-NAMING ASSESSMENT

Provide a sheet of letters in random order (one set of lower-case, one set of upper-case). Use some method of indicating the letters one by one—pointing or running a card under each—as the child names each letter. Do not help the child or indicate if he or she is right or wrong. Count the number of letters identified correctly. Discontinue testing if the child is unable to identify 10 consecutive capital letters.

PHONOLOGICAL AWARENESS ASSESSMENT

Identifying rhyme and beginning sounds are among the most fundamental tasks in the area of phonological awareness, and therefore practice should be administered to all children. However, if a child is not familiar with these concepts, discontinue testing.

Blending and segmenting onsets and rimes (see page 88) are more advanced phonemic awareness skills. Omit blending if a child is unable to identify beginning sounds. Omit segmenting if the child struggles with blending.

Blending and segmenting phonemes are among the most advanced phonemic awareness skills; use only with students who were successful with the onsets and rimes tasks.

Concepts-about-Print Assessment

Child's Name ______________________	*Nov*	*May*
Instructional Reading Level Knows where/what the cover of the book is		
Knows to read from front to back		
Knows the difference between text and pictures		
Knows what a letter is		
Knows what a word is		
Knows where to begin reading		
Tracks left to right		
Letter Naming Number of capital letters identified correctly		
Number of lower-case letters identified correctly		
Phonological Awareness Gives rhymes		
Hears beginning sounds		
Blends onsets and rimes		
Segments onsets and rimes		
Blends phonemes		
Segments phonemes		

Anecdotal Notes

Tell the student, "Flip through this book and tell me what you know about the words in the book." Jot your notes about the student's responses in the boxes below.

First Testing Period:	*Second Testing Period*

Sample Lesson for Emergent Readers

I selected the book *Sun Fun* (see page 57) for my emergent reading group.

Before Reading

I introduced the book by showing the cover and asking students to "show what they know" about the print. Fareeda noticed the capital "F" just like in her name. After Matthew identified the word "fun," several other students made the connection to "sun." I mentioned that "sun" and "fun" rhyme, and ask the students for other words that sound the same. The students offered "bun," "run," and "one." Later we added the *-un* family to the chunk chart.

I reviewed the title, *Sun Fun*, and told the students that the book was written by Elle Ruth Orav, and illustrated by Lam Quach. I told them the book's birthday was 2001.

To invite personal connections, I asked the students to tell what they do for fun in the sun, and I made an experience chart of their responses. Then I suggested that we read the book to see what the person in this story does for "sun fun." Before independent reading, we took a pic-flic to ensure that there was no unfamiliar vocabulary. I reinforced the phrase "I can put on...." The last line of the book does not follow the pattern, saying "I can have fun in the sun." I asked the students if they could match the words from the title and figure out the line. When they couldn't, I told them the line.

During Reading

I distributed the books and the tracking fingers (plastic "witch fingers" from the dollar store) and stagger started the reading while the rest of the students silently perused the pictures. I circulated among the students to listen to them read.

When Jared read "I can put on my cowboy hat" instead of "sun hat," I reminded him to take a look at the starting letter of "sun."

When Carly read "I can put on my shoes" instead of "sandals," I asked her to "look across the word" to attend to more than just the initial sound.

After Reading

After reading, we got out our word framers (magnifying glasses from the party favors section of the dollar store) and looked for the words *I*, *can*, *put*, *on*, and *my*. We matched word cards to the words in the text, then I added these cards to a collection of high-frequency words we had already studied.

The students enjoyed playing a quick game of Bang!, which involves identifying words in isolation. Among the collection of word cards are three or four cards that say *Bang!* Students pass the deck around the circle and take turns drawing a card. If they can read the word on the card, they get to keep it. If they draw the Bang card, they have to return all their cards to the deck.

As an independent activity after reading, the students made "Snow Fun" take-home books using the pattern "I can put on my...." They read their books to one another and took them home to read to their families.

Working with emergent readers can provide some of the most rewarding teaching and learning experiences you will ever have. The delight of these students as they begin to "crack the code," their growing confidence in themselves as readers and writers, and the enthusiasm with which they tackle learning tasks is not found with any other group. Where else would you hear a young reader exclaim with delight at the end of a shared reading experience, "We can read!"

7 Guided Reading for Early Readers

Andrew loves to read and write, and enjoys talking about books and stories. He recognizes a large number of familiar words on sight and can sound out many more. His prize purchase at the last school book fair was a dictionary. "Do you know what word is in here?" he chortled gleefully. "Underpants!"

Andrew is an early reader. He has a strong sense of how print works, including the understanding that words are separate units. He reads word by word, tracking his reading with his finger. Like most early readers, he has developed a sense of story and can retell what he has read. Unlike the emergent reading stage, which relies mostly on memory and pictures, the early reading level is the beginning of real "reading work."

Ironically, one of the mixed blessings of this stage is the students' newfound knowledge of graphophonics. Once they learn how to decode, many early readers rely so heavily on sounding out letters that they lose meaning in what they read. This happens particularly when readers attend to only the beginning and ending sounds of the words. So it is important for the teacher to guide students in the flexible use of a variety of cueing strategies for word solving.

Early readers

- will engage in discussion about what is read
- begin to apply letter–sound correspondences to decoding, especially initial and final sounds
- have an increasing repertoire of high-frequency words
- understand one-to-one correspondence
- read word by word, using tracking
- have solid concepts about print
- rely less on pictures as a cueing strategy

The Guided Reading Lesson for Early Readers

Early readers are just beginning to read conventionally and still require a lot of teacher support and scaffolding to develop independent reading strategies. Ideally, groups should consist of no more than four to six students, and you should try to meet with these groups three or four times a week. Texts for early readers are short; a 15- to 20-minute lesson should enable you to complete an entire text with these students.

Areas of focus for early readers include the following:

- using cueing systems flexibly to solve unfamiliar words
- applying letter–sound correspondences efficiently
- retelling stories—comprehension and story structure
- developing an increasing repertoire of high-frequency words
- self-monitoring comprehension and self-correcting miscues

Flexible use of cueing strategies is an important focus for early readers. We want to support their increasing mastery of letter–sound correspondences, especially with letter combinations and patterns such as word families. We also want to ensure that they integrate the use of graphophonics with other cueing strategies such as meaning and syntax.

In addition to word study, we want to encourage students to apply the comprehension strategies they have learned with read-alouds and shared reading to reading that they are doing themselves. Retelling stories reinforces knowledge of story structure, encourages summarizing, and builds the foundation for more complex understanding and inference at later stages.

Appropriate Texts for Early Readers

Texts for early readers support the newly independent reader. Rather than simply labeling pictures, these texts have simple plots and familiar concepts and structures. The text is dominated by high-frequency words and decodable words. When new vocabulary is introduced, it is repeated over and over throughout the text for reinforcement. Although these texts lack the heavy patterns of the emergent-level text, the sentences are short and simple.

In texts for early readers

- the print is large, though the print placement on the page may vary
- language structures are choppy and stilted
- there are mostly short, simple sentences with fewer repetitive sentence patterns
- there is increasing use of punctuation conventions, such as question marks and quotation marks
- there are line breaks at meaningful phrases
- illustrations provide support for the story, but may not give explicit clues for decoding
- there is use of direct speech
- there may be multiple lines of print on the page
- new vocabulary is repeated frequently.
- we find simple story lines, sometimes with surprise endings
- plots are mainly based on realistic situations that students are likely to experience

The following is an example of a typical early-level text:

Baby Canada Goose Flies South written by Janet Intscher, illustrated by Rebecca Buchanan; Curriculum Plus, 2001. Reprinted with permission.

What the Lesson Looks Like

BEFORE READING: BOOK INTRODUCTION

Rereading familiar books is a good way to start every Guided Reading lesson. It provides bulk reading practice and establishes effective routines for the lesson that ease transitions from other activities. As with emergent readers, ensure that each student has a collection of previously read books to read before the formal lesson starts. Book boxes (see page 49) are ideal for holding three or four early-level books.

Introduce the cover information and provide a one- or two-sentence overview. Invite students to make connections to their own personal experiences. This is a good time to teach students to share ideas with their reading partners. You might say, "Turn to the person beside you and tell them what this title reminds you of."

The picture walk, or pic-flic, for early readers will not be as extensive as for emergent readers. Preview only those pages that present potentially challenging vocabulary or concepts, and model any language patterns that the students will need to know in order to access the text. Also introduce anchor words. Remember that the purpose of the preview is to provide enough scaffolding for the students to be able to read most of the text on their own with the strategies and knowledge they already have.

Anchor words are the high-frequency words that "glue" the text together.

As a final step in the book introduction, you may want to use an "I wonder…" statement, to set a purpose for reading and to invite students to predict what may happen in the book. A statement like, "I wonder what will happen at the park" sets both a context and a purpose for reading.

DURING READING: SCAFFOLDED READING

The during-reading portion of the lesson is when the readers apply their new-found knowledge and strategies to reading actual texts. Once again, each student will read the text independently. Early readers still need to be reading aloud; however, this is a time to emphasize whisper reading so they can begin to rely less on the actual auditory feedback and more on the voice in their heads. Continue using a stagger start to discourage reading in chorus. Encourage students to track words and lines with a finger, mini pointer, or other tool.

As the children read, offer support as needed, focusing on cueing strategies: meaning, syntax, and graphophonics. When your students make miscues, your first task is to resist the temptation to intervene on the spot! Remember that your goal is to build independent readers. You want your students to learn to monitor their own miscues, not to rely you to maintain their accuracy.

Since many early readers have a tendency to fixate on phonics, we need to remind them that the whole purpose of reading is to make sense of print. When you hear a student make a miscue, and he or she does not correct it, ask first, "Does that make sense?" This forces the reader to attend to the meaning of the text. Often the miscue *does* make sense; in fact, skilful readers, including adults, make these sorts of miscues all the time. In most cases, we don't even bother to correct miscues that don't interfere with meaning. However, this is reading instruction and we want our students to focus on accuracy as well as comprehension. Guide the students to use all of their cueing strategies whether or not the miscue makes sense in the passage.

If the miscue makes sense, the next question is "Does it sound right?" This forces the reader to focus on syntax, how our language goes together. It involves listening for whether the groups of words that are read sound like they would if we were saying them in speech. Students with a strong oral language base do not make many miscues that are syntactically incorrect.

The final question should be, "Does it look right?" In other words, do the sounds of the word that was read match the letters on the page? Talk about the miscue that was read and how to accurately apply knowledge of letter–sound correspondences.

Other word-level prompts for early readers include

- "Do you see any chunks inside the word?
- "Does this word remind you of any other word you know?"
- "Take a running start."
- "Slide into the word."
- "Take a guess and see if it works."
- "Just say 'blank' and read on to see if the rest of the sentence helps you."

Tip

When early readers make a miscue, ask these three questions:

- ***"Does it make sense?"***
- ***"Does it sound right?"***
- ***"Does it look right?"***

Andrew's early reading group was reading the book *All Clean*, by Jo Winsor. At one point, the text read, "Marion cleaned the parrot's cage," but Andrew read, "Marion cleaned the parrot's feathers." After pausing to allow Andrew an opportunity to self-correct, I asked him to go back and reread the sentence. "Does that make sense?" It did; even the illustration depicted the vacuum cleaner poking through the bars of the cage, ruffling the parrot's feathers. "Does it sound right?" Sure. Andrew had substituted the noun "cage" with another noun, "feathers."

But when we asked, "Does it look right?" the answer was "no." I asked Andrew, "What sound do we hear at the beginning of 'feathers'? If the word was 'feathers,' what letter would we see?" After establishing that there was no *f* in this word, I asked Andrew to focus on the initial sound of the word in "cage," and to guess again. When he determined that the correct word was "cage," together we made sure it fulfilled all the criteria—it made sense, sounded right, and matched the print.

Working with students in this way enables you to keep track of what cueing strategies they are using and which they are confusing, thereby enabling you to plan instruction to meet the needs of each group. Andrew's miscues, in the case described here, are an indication to the teacher that he is ready for more work on word families. A pattern of miscues such as confusing "shorted" for "shouted" informs the teacher that this student has a good grasp of beginning and ending sounds but needs to attend to medial sounds.

AFTER READING

As always, after-reading activities should be carefully chosen to build reading proficiency and higher-level thinking. Take note of strategies you observed your students using as they were reading. Take advantage of opportunities to present brief mini lessons on strategies and word solving.

Because stories at the early reading level have simple plots, this is a good time to begin discussions of plot lines and literary elements. Rereading the text and dramatizing the story through readers theatre provide reading practice. Guided discussion supports and extends higher-level thinking.

Oral retelling of the story should be a key element of the after-reading discussion at the early-reading stage, now that the texts have simple story lines. Retelling enables the students to pay attention to overall meaning, story structure, and the distinction between key ideas and supporting details. It also lays a foundation for more complex texts and inferential comprehension.

Teaching Emphases to Use with Early Readers

Retelling

Retelling is both a comprehension strategy and an assessment strategy. It encourages the reader to attend to the meaning of the text, reinforces elements of story structure (such as characters, setting, and plot), requires readers to distinguish between key ideas and supporting details, and encourages oral language development. It also reveals to the teacher what the students understand and remember about the story, and what they know about story structure and literary language.

It is important to teach students how to retell a story and what will be expected of their retelling.

Group retellings of read-alouds and shared book experiences can build comprehension strategies and understanding of story elements. Graphic organizers or props, such as pictures or puppets, may also be used to aid retelling. For more ideas for teaching Retelling, see Chapter 12 on Comprehension Instruction in the Guided Reading program.

Letter Patterns

Your early readers have mastered all of the consonant sounds and many vowel sounds. Now you want to reinforce vowel sounds and build on knowledge of letter patterns.

Word building is an activity in which children manipulate letters to make words, starting with small words and increasing until a word is made with all of the letters. By guiding children in building, sorting, and transferring words, we teach and reinforce many types of letter patterns, from rimes and onsets to consonant blends and digraphs. More information on building words and other techniques for teaching word families is found in Chapter 10 on Phonics Instruction in the Guided Reading program.

Story Structure

Texts for early readers start to tell complete stories, so this is a good time to begin using terms like *character* and *problem*. We also want to draw students' attention to the structures of dialogue—quotation marks, tag lines, speech balloons.

Sample Lesson for Early Readers

My early-reading group recently read *Baby Canada Goose Flies South* (see page 66). My objectives for the lesson were to review high-frequency words, reinforce retelling, and introduce dialogue structures.

Before Reading

When I held up the book cover, my students immediately identified the Canada Geese on the cover. Jessica was able to read most of the title to us, but was stumped by "south." This was a good opportunity to introduce the strategy of "looking into the word" to see any patterns or little words that are already known. The beginning and ending sounds were easy, and once we identified the little word "out" in the word, we knew the vowel sound as well. Now my students were able to make a text-to-world connection, as we charted everything they knew about geese flying south for the winter.

Before the picture walk, I reviewed some high-frequency words that were already on the wall by playing Guess the Covered Word. For this activity, I put the word card into a pocket and reveal one letter at a time while the students try to predict what the word is.

Our pic-flic was brief, as the book contains few difficult words or concepts for these students. Variations of the word "fly" are repeated throughout the book, so I made sure to point out the words "fly," "flies," and "flew." We also worked together to decode the word "cried." Then we looked at a few pictures to make predictions about the story.

During Reading

I distributed the books and stagger started the reading, asking the students to read to find out what happens when Baby Goose flies south.

As my students read, I circulated around the room offering support as needed. My goal is to encourage self-monitoring, so I had to discipline myself to wait for the student to self-correct before intervening! They have heard me ask the three questions—Does it make sense? Does it sound right? Does it match the print?—so many times that now I want them to ask themselves those questions.

After Reading

After reading, we collaboratively retell the story, using the 5-W (Who, What, When, Where, Why) structure. We revisit the "talking parts" and identify quotation marks and tag lines. Together we create sentences from the following prompts:

Baby Goose cried, " ____ "
Father Goose said, " ____ "

I provided the story as a readers theatre script, so the students enjoyed the opportunity to practise and perform the reading for their classmates.

The early reader has just begun to discover the power that comes with negotiating sounds, letters, words, and sentences. We can support that empowerment by encouraging students to focus on meaning. Within the rest of the balanced literacy program, we are building writing skills, extending understanding of letter–sound relationships through word families and letter clusters, enhancing higher-level thinking through read-alouds, and encouraging fluency and confidence through plenty of opportunities for rereading independent level texts.

8 Guided Reading for Developing Readers

Tyler likes to pick chapter books for free-time reading. He takes pride in the fact that it takes him only two or three days to complete a book. Tyler usually chooses books from the same series, but will read any mystery book. Word recognition is no longer an issue for Tyler, so he can focus on the ideas and concepts. Tyler recently reported that he was able to solve the mystery in his book before the main character figured it out!

Tyler is a developing reader. He has a large bank of high-frequency words and uses cueing strategies quite flexibly and efficiently. Because word solving is a less critical issue for him, he is able to access meaning in longer texts.

We sometimes consider readers like Tyler to be in transition—making the transition from a focus on decoding to a focus on comprehension, the transition from oral reading to silent reading, and the transition from word-by-word reading to fluent phrasing.

Developing readers are becoming increasingly confident and independent in their reading strategies. They can understand and retell a story. They have a sense of story structure, which they apply to predicting and comprehending the text. They are able to relate to stories and characters beyond their personal realm of experience. This is the stage at which folk tales, science fiction, fantasy, and other imaginative texts may be introduced. Students also become more aware of non-fiction texts and can use their reading strategies to learn new ideas. At this level, readers need support as they extend their thinking and their comprehension beyond the literal level.

Developing readers

- understand and apply story structure
- can sustain attention for longer texts
- are aware of different genres
- attend to overall meaning of text
- begin to monitor their own comprehension
- can get information from books
- can access appropriate-level informational texts
- have a strong repertoire of high-frequency words
- are able to solve many unfamiliar words
- can appreciate imaginative concepts and characters
- will make inferences, with guidance

The Guided Reading Lesson for Developing Readers

Because developing readers require less support than emergent and early readers, the groups may be larger, up to six or eight students. It is a good idea to establish reading partners within the group, for discussion and collaboration. Groups at this level should meet with the teacher two or three times a week for strategy instruction. The rest of their time should be spent on reading practice. At this stage, students may be introduced to literature discussion groups, which operate with minimal teacher involvement.

Because texts for developing readers are longer, they often are not completed in one lesson. Sometimes students must learn to take responsibility for completing the text independently in preparation for a Guided Reading lesson.

Areas of focus for developing readers include the following:

- silent reading
- fluency and expression
- making inferences
- summarizing and synthesizing
- self-monitoring and correction
- revisiting the text for additional information or confirmation
- written and oral responses

Beginning readers need auditory feedback to guide them in their reading, but developing readers are making the transition from oral to silent reading. At this stage, we want our students to learn to hear that voice in their heads; most of the reading they will do throughout school and life will be silent reading.

There is extensive research to support a correlation between fluent reading and comprehension (National Reading Panel, 2000). Comprehension of longer texts is impeded when readers are negotiating word by word.

Part of the transition from oral to silent reading involves the development of reading fluency. We want to wean students of the habit of tracking word by word; now we want to encourage natural phrasing and expression.

As texts become more complex, it is no longer adequate to invite students to simply make predictions and connections before reading, then forget about them until they have finished reading. If predicting is to be a useful reading strategy, the reader must continue to confirm and adjust predictions, as he or she acquires new information throughout the reading. Similarly, making connections and accessing schema should be an ongoing process in order to support the reader's comprehension.

Now we want our students to move beyond literal comprehension and develop higher-level thinking. We must begin to reinforce the strategies of confirming or rejecting predictions, making inferences, and synthesizing information that we have already introduced through classroom read-alouds. The scaffolds we provide at this stage will provide the foundation for independence in the next stage.

Appropriate Texts for Developing Readers

Texts for developing readers have much more variety than those for earlier levels. Illustrations are usually present, but they enhance the story rather than offering support for decoding. Sentences are longer, but usually still sound somewhat choppy. Story lines are much more complex, often having several characters or episodes. This is the stage at which readers are likely to encounter imaginative texts such as folk tales or fantasy; now they have developed the maturity to see beyond their own personal experiences.

Tip

Encourage developing readers to "fall in love" with a series. This will give them a range of books to choose for independent reading that they know they will be able to read and enjoy.

Series books such as *Frog and Toad* or *Junie B. Jones* are popular with developing readers. Familiar characters, concepts, and text structures offer comfort to the reader who is just beginning to demonstrate independence in reading.

Humor and rhyming text have great appeal at this stage. Rhyming text is often quite challenging for beginning readers because it tends to contain language structures not present in speech patterns. However, even the youngest children can appreciate listening to rhyming text and, by the developing reader stage, they have the strategies in place to read it.

Texts for developing readers

- may contain imaginative concepts, themes, and characters
- comprise a variety of forms and genres
- have illustrations that enhance the story line
- do not repeat and reinforce new vocabulary
- may contain rhyming text
- have more print on each page
- contain longer sentences, but often are still choppy
- have text in block paragraphs
- use a variety of fonts, and may contain unique text features
- have complex, developed story lines with multiple episodes

Here is a typical story for developing readers:

Sara thought fast. "When I turned on the computer, smoke came out. So I called the fire department! They put out the fire, but the computer is a big mess. And my dad is kind of mad."

8

"The fire department?" all the kids said.

9

What a Story! By Paul Kropp, illustrated by Loris Lesynski (Scholastic Canada, 2002). Reprinted with permission from Paul Kropp and Loris Lesynski

What the Lesson Looks Like

BEFORE READING: BOOK INTRODUCTION

A book's dedication may be interesting to students, and young writers often like to include dedications in their own writing. You may want to talk about why writers sometimes dedicate their stories to a special person.

Here, as with other stages, the book introduction is intended to provide the necessary scaffolding and background information for students to access the text with the strategies that they already have. Present the title, author, illustrator, and any other publication information you feel is of interest and relevance to the students. The publication date can sometimes be a key bit of information, particularly for informational texts.

This is also the time to introduce key vocabulary that students may not know and will need in order to understand the story. How do you decide what words to introduce ahead of time? First, you want to select words that are germane to

It is unlikely that you will undertake a picture walk, or pic-flic, at this stage. You will probably read the book in sections, and address specific pages as needed during the reading.

understanding the story. Then, determine whether the text provides enough support for the student to determine the meaning of the word from the context. When possible, allow the students to word solve for themselves. If you feel there is not enough support in the text for students to understand a particular word, pre-teach that word. (For more ideas on vocabulary instruction, see Chapter 11.)

Prior knowledge and personal connections are important contexts for comprehension, and should be addressed in the book introduction. Until now, we have tended to focus on students' connections to their own lives and experiences. As children mature, however, they are increasingly able to connect to the world around them. You may want to ask students to think about connections to other books or to big ideas, such as friendship, poverty, or war. Keene and Zimmerman (1998) tell us that readers make three types of connections: text-to-self, text-to-text, and text-to-world. (For a discussion on how making connections aids comprehension, see Chapter 12.)

As we continue to help our students build strategic independence, we want them to understand that they should read in different ways for different purposes. Making predictions about what the text will be about is one way of setting a purpose for reading, because it focuses the reader's attention on whether the text will provide the information we expect it to. Predictions also enhance the ability to make inferences, because they involve combining what we know about the text with what is already in our heads.

Making connections, predictions, and inferences are not ends in themselves. We teach students to do these things in order to help them understand what they read. It is important to make that purpose explicit. The developing-reader stage is a good time to start to develop metacognition, that is, to ensure that students begin thinking about their thinking. In order to "make it metacognitive", it is important to discuss the ways readers confirm and adjust predictions and connections as they acquire new information throughout the reading; the ongoing process of making connections and accessing schema helps readers understand what they read.

DURING READING: SCAFFOLDED READING

The scaffolded reading component for developing readers will look somewhat different than it does in earlier stages. Because the texts are usually longer, you are unlikely to complete the entire book in one sitting. You may take two or three sessions to complete a text, or you may guide students through portions of the text and leave the rest for them to read independently.

At this stage, encourage students to read silently, in their heads. Even those who still need to vocalize can be encouraged to "say" the words silently to themselves.

In my class, developing readers know that one of their jobs is to bring a clipboard, pencil, and notebook to the Guided Reading lesson. I also provide them with a Reading Tool Kit.

THE READING TOOL KIT

The base of the Reading Tool Kit is a narrow folder; these are made from a laminated file folder cut into strips about 10 cm wide. On each narrow folder are a variety of sticky notes, usually about six of each, ranging in size from squares to "fringes" (large sticky notes cut in strips almost to the end, to tear off when small pieces are needed.) One note is a STOP sign, for use when I want students to stop reading after a certain portion of the text. The top of the folder has a coil large enough to hold a pencil.

Independent reading strategies and higher-level thinking are the focus for developing readers. Usually, we read a portion of the text at a time, in order to attend to a particular strategy. I tell the students to place their STOP signs at a certain point in the text and read till they get to it. Depending on the strategy we are using, I might ask them to put a sticky strip under words that are new or interesting. Or I might have them write a connection or question on a square sticky note placed at strategic points.

Tip

Sticky notes are an essential reading tool for developing readers and beyond.

> Wilfred Burton likes to use the "I Wonder. . ." code with his students as they read fiction text. He tells his students that all good readers wonder about things as they read, and models his own wonderings during read-alouds and Guided Reading by thinking out loud about his reading processes.
>
> Wilfred has his students put question marks on small sticky notes to represent I Wonder points. He then asks them to place an I Wonder at any spot that confuses them or makes them curious.
>
> After they have finished reading, they all discuss their I Wonders and talk about whether their questions were answered in the reading. He helps them develop strategies for fixing up points of confusion in their reading, and helps them distinguish creating suspense from problems in reading.
>
> The "I Wonder. . ." code requires students to monitor their own comprehension. It teaches them to attend to aspects of the text that confuse them, and they become more alert to consciously self-correcting that confusion. Knowing that even grown-up readers sometimes wonder as they read is a good reminder that effective readers are always thinking about their thinking.

Here are some ways you can suggest students use sticky notes during scaffolded reading:

- Put a note under any words you find interesting or unfamiliar.
- Put a note with a question mark beside things you don't understand or wonder about.
- Every time you make a connection, write it on a sticky note and place it in the appropriate spot.
- Respond to "stop and think" points that have been marked throughout the reading.

Students can share their notes with their reading partners until the others are finished reading. Together, discuss the notes the students made and where they placed them. Remind students of how this strategy can help them when they read on their own.

AFTER READING: DISCUSSION/INSTRUCTION/EXTENSION

No matter what after-reading activities are used, it is important that they extend our students' thinking skills and build reading proficiency. Developing readers should be encouraged to extend their reading experiences through writing as well as discussion.

Discussion remains one of the most productive after-reading activities. During reading, address strategy use. After reading, focus on metacognition:

- "What strategy did you use when you didn't understand that part?"
- "In what ways did you change your predictions as you read?"
- "How did your connections help you understand as you read?"

We must always think about our purpose in introducing any activity, to ensure that our students are receiving the most educational benefit.

Encourage students to revisit the text to find support for their ideas and responses. Skimming and scanning should be taught and practised. Invite students' opinions and evaluations, but always ask for evidence from the text.

After-reading activities for developing readers include

- writing a sequel or a new ending to the story
- dramatizing the story through readers theatre, improvisation, or role drama
- sketching a story map of key elements of the story

As always, let's not forget that the very best follow up to reading is...more reading! One of the most important activities we can do at this stage is to help our students develop reading fluency.

Teaching Emphases to Use with Developing Readers

Revisiting the Text

"I don't have a reason. I just liked it." Teaching students not just to read critically, but also to provide reasons for their opinions, is a challenging task for teachers. The SOS Response, described on page 133, invites students to summarize what they have read, give an opinion, and provide support for their opinion.

Building Reading Fluency through Readers Theatre

Readers theatre scripts are available commercially and on many Internet sites. However, it is easy to develop your own scripts from Guided Reading texts, and sometimes students will be able to create scripts themselves.

It may seem ironic that fluency practice is emphasized at a stage when we are encouraging students to read silently. Efficient silent reading depends on fluency, but oral reading is necessary in order to practise and assess fluency. Performance reading is the best way to encourage students to read fluently and expressively. Readers theatre is a strategy that involves performing from a script. Few, if any, gestures, props, or costumes are required; the focus is on performance of the voice.

Sample Lesson for Developing Readers

I selected the book *What a Story!* by Paul Kropp (see page 73) for my developing readers group. At 42 pages, this book is too long for one lesson, but broken up into two or three sections it was quite manageable for these students.

Before Reading

After introducing the title, author, and illustrator of the book, I told the students that this is a book about a girl named Sara who has trouble writing stories in school, so she makes up amazing excuses for why she didn't do her writing. I asked the students to turn to their reading partners and share the hardest part about writing stories for them.

This story contains many three-syllable words, so it was a good time to introduce the strategy of breaking words into syllables for decoding. I demonstrated to students how big words like "department," "computer," "hurricane," and "imagine" can be decoded in parts. I also reviewed the strategy of looking inside the word for recognizable word parts or even little words.

During Reading

I distributed the books and the Reading Tool Kits. I asked the students to take three sticky strips for underlining hard words they encountered as they read, so we could revisit these after reading. I told the students to flip to page 10 and put their STOP signs at the end of the page. That is how far we would read that day.

To begin, I read the first page aloud while the students followed. This set the humorous tone of the story and presented the teacher's name. I also introduced the names of the other characters. Then I suggested that the students read to page 10 to find out what Sara says when she has trouble writing a story.

Most of the students were reading silently by this stage, so I observed their reading behaviors and asked them to read passages aloud to me for individual support. For example, when Natalie said "fire compartment," I asked her to look at the word "computer" and see if they had the same starting syllable.

After Reading

After reading, we discussed the words the students underlined with their sticky strips, and what strategies they used to solve those words.

I also wanted the students to go back into the story to find information, so I asked them to find the parts that answer the following questions:

- What did George write about?
- What happened to the computer?
- How did Sara's Dad feel?
- What didn't Sara like about her teacher?

Because I wanted the students to start thinking inferentially, I asked them these questions:

1. Why do you think Sara said the fire department might give her a medal?
2. Can you find the part that tells that in the text?
3. How can you get the answer to that question?

With the time left in the lesson, I asked the students to put their STOP signs at the end of page 20 and read to that point. We would discuss and read on during a subsequent lesson.

After completing the entire book, I had the students write a written response to this question: What excuse do you think Sara could give the next time she had trouble with her homework?

Developing readers are well on their way to confidence and competence. They can decode words and comprehend meaning. They can retell stories and recognize different genres. They can get information as well as enjoyment from reading. Now our role is to refine their reading strategies, to encourage inference and higher-level thinking, to enable students to access increasingly challenging texts without our assistance.

9 Guided Reading for Fluent Readers

Corey has just gone on his first plane trip and he is fascinated by flying. On library days, he heads straight for the non-fiction section of the library, where he chooses a pile of information books on planes, rockets, and air travel. A confident reader, Corey knows how to choose books that are just right for him, but if there's a difficult book that particularly interests him, he has the strategies and confidence in place to give it a try.

Corey is a fluent reader, at a stage that will extend throughout his school career and into adulthood. He has a wide repertoire of comprehension strategies, but will continue to refine and build on them, as well as extending his knowledge, thinking skills, and experiences with a wide range of text forms at increasing levels of difficulty.

Obviously, the fluent reader stage spans a huge range of skills, strategies, and experience with print. Although the strategies of effective readers are somewhat similar whether the reader is seven or seventeen, the needs of a fluent reader at the end of Grade 2 are quite different than those of an adolescent or an adult. Throughout the school years, teachers have a responsibility to provide instruction that offers exposure to increasingly difficult texts in a wide variety of genres, and to continue to refine strategy use and encourage higher-level thinking.

Fluent readers are beginning to read with fluency—and much more. They have the strategies and knowledge to access a wide variety of text genres. They are able to take risks with challenging vocabulary. They are beginning to go beyond literal interpretations of text to analyze, synthesize, interpret, and evaluate what they read. In other words, they are well on their way to becoming strategic, independent readers.

When reading appropriate level texts, fluent readers

- use many sources of information for decoding and comprehension
- are willing to take risks with more difficult texts
- self-monitor comprehension during reading
- rarely make miscues that interfere with meaning
- have strategies to tackle challenging vocabulary
- make inferences, evaluations, and interpretations of texts
- revisit texts to provide support for ideas
- understand and respect differing points of view
- read with fluency and phrasing
- sustain interest and attention in lengthy texts
- can access a variety of genres for information and pleasure

The Guided Reading Lesson for Fluent Readers

Although fluent readers are becoming independent and require less support than those in earlier stages, it is still important to provide regular strategy instruction. Not only do fluent readers still need to build and refine their repertoire of reading strategies, they need to be scaffolded to use these strategies with increasingly difficult texts.

Group size for fluent readers may extend to eight to ten members. The group may meet with the teacher only once or twice a week for intensive strategy instruction, depending on their age and level of independence. Of course, they are still also receiving teacher attention in other components of the balanced literacy program. We mustn't forget that, even though the students may be increasingly effective readers, their level of independence is still only that of a seven- or eight-year-old.

Because of the wide range of learners and texts at this level, the structure of the Guided Reading lesson may vary more than at other levels. Depending on the type and complexity of the text, the students may be asked to complete an independent activity that introduces the book or sets the context for reading. The Guided Reading lesson would then focus on scaffolding the students through a complete short text or portions of a longer text. Or, the teacher may use Guided Reading sessions to introduce the reading and the strategy, then have the students read the text independently. Some teachers like to integrate literature circles with strategic instruction, alternating strategy work with book discussion. Another alternative is to extend one text over several Guided Reading sessions, as long as there is not too much time between sessions.

Areas of focus for fluent readers may include the following:

- metacognition: when, why, and how to use reading strategies
- introducing new genres and revisiting familiar text forms
- teaching literary elements
- self-questioning and self-monitoring
- predicting and confirming during reading
- visualizing
- distinguishing main ideas and supporting details
- coping with challenging vocabulary and texts
- extending higher-level thinking
- making the reading–writing connection
- examining one's own reading habits
- recognizing and appreciating different points of view
- revisiting strategies from previous levels, as needed

At all stages, but particularly with fluent readers, it is essential to focus on metacognition—thinking about thinking. Whenever we discuss or apply a strategy, we talk about how that strategy has helped us read, and under what circumstances we might use that strategy again.

Appropriate Texts for Fluent Readers

Tip

When a child can read 90–95% of the words in a text, that text is at the optimal level of difficulty for teaching that student, or instructional level, because it has the right balance of support and challenge.

The range of texts for fluent readers is as extensive as the stage itself. We have to remind ourselves that it is just as important to find instructional-level texts for fluent readers as it is for emergent and early readers. Use oral reading records and readability tools to find independent- and instructional-level texts for these students as well.

Almost any type of text is appropriate for fluent readers. Probably the main thing that sets apart fluent-level text from earlier levels is the presence of literary language. Here we find figurative, descriptive language that defies literal interpretation. Concepts are more abstract and may require more inference and interpretation. Sentence length and complexity are other key indicators of fluent-level texts; the more embedded clauses, the more difficult a sentence is to negotiate.

Texts for fluent readers generally contain

- literary language and challenging vocabulary
- a story line that contains many episodes and extends over a long time period
- a variety of genres
- concepts beyond the reader's realm of experience
- a variety of sentence lengths and structures
- standard-sized print, with more variety in page layout
- few or no illustrations; entire pages of print

Virtually any text is suitable for fluent-level readers; here is an excerpt from a good example.

"Mom's from Mars." I shrugged my shoulders and rolled my eyes.

Janet, the only friend I have — and this year she doesn't even go to the same school — sat across from me at the table. She nodded in sympathy.

Slip, slap, slip, slap. Martian Mom shuffled past us. She didn't say "Hello" or "How are you girls?" Not the custom on Mars. Mom opened the fridge door.

She stood there for a minute in her towelly robe, with her hair standing at attention like little spikes or antennae. Yeah, she came from outer space all right.

Her eyes didn't blink. They

Tiger Catcher's Kid by Sylvia McNicoll; Nelson Canada, 1989. Reprinted with permission.

What the Lesson Looks Like

BEFORE READING: BOOK INTRODUCTION

After introducing the title, author, and publication information, you may or may not choose to invite connections and predictions, depending on the objectives for the lesson. Fluent readers should be learning to adjust their reading style and rate according to the purpose for reading.

Gloria Antifaiff uses a racing analogy when she teaches students about adjusting reading rate and style. She tells students that when they are reading a difficult book or a book that is heavily loaded with facts, they will want to *walk* through the book; that is, go slowly and read every word and sentence carefully. When they are reading for pleasure, they might *jog* through the book, reading in chunks and phrases. When they want to get a general sense of what a book or section is about, or see if it contains the information they want, they might *race* through that text.

She carefully models each style of reading, and has the students practise them and talk about different purposes for each. She pays particular attention to racing through the book, showing students how they can *skim* for an overview of the text, *scan* to look for specific information, and even *skip* information that doesn't serve their purpose.

The book introduction will vary according to the nature of the text and the objectives of the lesson. Opportunities should be provided for accessing prior knowledge and setting purposes for reading, particularly with informational texts (see Chapter 14 for more on using non-fiction in Guided Reading). At this time, you should guide the students in establishing a context for reading and introduce key vocabulary that students may not be able to access on their own. (See Chapter 11 for strategies for introducing vocabulary.)

DURING READING: SCAFFOLDED READING

The during-reading component of the lesson always focuses on scaffolding readers in strategy use as you guide students through a text. Be sure to provide a balance of short texts in a variety of genres with longer texts, such as novels and chapter books.

If the text is too long to read in one sitting, have students read sections at a time. Use sticky-note STOP signs to remind the students to stop at strategic points. At these stopping points, you might ask them to self-question, to visualize, or to confirm or adjust their predictions, depending on your objectives for the lesson.

Because group size is likely to be larger than at previous levels, you will want to take advantage of reading partners for discussion. This gives students opportunities to share their ideas and makes them accountable for participating in the dialogue. Some responses to the reading may be written and some will be oral; be sure to provide opportunities to discuss written responses.

Whenever you ask basic comprehension questions, require students to find the answer or the evidence in the story. Revisiting the text to access information is an important reading activity.

Encourage students to go back to the text to find support for ideas or opinions. Of course, at this stage, they will be reading silently, so this is a good opportunity to integrate fluency practice: invite students to "read the sentence/paragraph/section that tells…."

The best way to teach and practise inferential thinking is through guided discussion and questioning. Through effective questioning, you can extend your students' thinking; however, this is the time to make those habits independent, so the students will analyze, synthesize, and interpret their reading when you are not there to scaffold them. Teach students how to ask themselves questions as they read, using the I Wonder strategy described in Chapter 8 or Three-Level Questioning strategies from Chapter 12.

AFTER READING

Much of the discussion and strategy building of the lesson will take place during the scaffolded reading. Any extension activities should be carefully selected to help extend the students' reading, writing, and thinking. At this stage, students should be able to communicate their thoughts in writing, so written responses that apply strategies and extend thinking may be used as a follow-up to reading, depending on the learning objectives of the lesson.

In addition to comprehension strategies, fluent readers should begin to attend to elements of literature, such as characters, plot, theme, and literary language.

Teaching Emphases to Use with Fluent Readers

Synthesizing

Synthesizing is a reading strategy that helps readers comprehend and retain material they read by transforming it into a new form. Whether this transformation takes the form of a summary, a personal response, or a new form such as a poem or picture, it requires the reader to synthesize what he or she already knows with the new learning. Some alternatives for responding to reading may be found in Chapter 13.

Analyzing Literary Elements

Characterization, plot development, and theme are aspects of literary form that fluent readers should be able to identify and discuss. Activities like plot profiles help readers graphically depict the rising action in a narrative. Character analysis helps readers understand how character development moves a story along and how the author reveals the character's traits to us.

Identifying Writer's Craft

Tip

Read a text first for meaning, then have the students revisit it to look at the writer's craft. Tell them to note words and phrases that evoke images or emotions or capture their attention for some reason.

Texts for fluent readers are distinguishable from other levels by the evidence of literary, or "book," language and other elements of literary craft. At this stage, we would like teachers to pay attention to what the writer does to create mood, inspire visual images, and convey a message to the reader. The tools of the writer's craft include figurative language, comparisons such as similes and metaphors, foreshadowing, and evoking questions in the reader's mind. If we want our students to write effectively, we need to be more explicit in drawing their attention to powerful writing in books.

Writers often choose or combine words in particularly effective ways to convey images or evoke emotions. We not only want our students to recognize and appreciate this craft, we also want them to apply similar techniques in their own writing.

What Do You Notice? (see page 83) is an activity that encourages readers to take note of effective language and to practise using it. I use the example "the syrup of darkness" from the book *Twilight Comes Twice* by Ralph Fletcher. I tell the students I notice this phrase because it makes an unusual comparison of darkness to syrup. It gives me a mind picture of darkness being thick and slow-moving. I might call it "comparing two things that usually don't go together." If I were to try this literary technique, I might write "The cold air caught my breath like a stick of peppermint gum."

What Do You Notice?

Text and author:

Quote:

Why did you notice it?

What would you call it?

Try it yourself…

Sample Lesson for Fluent Readers

One of my fluent-level groups recently read *The True Story of the Three Little Pigs by A. Wolf*, as told to Jon Scieszka; Puffin, 1996.

Before Reading

The students enjoyed my story of hearing Jon Scieszka say that we can always remember his name because it rhymes with "Fresca." Together, we speculated on why the book is "as told to" Jon Scieszka rather than "by" Jon Scieszka.

We looked at the cover and noted that it looked like a newspaper page. We made a text-to-text connection by retelling the traditional story of "The Three Little Pigs," to ensure that the students remembered all the details. I invited observations about what kind of book it is, and we recalled titles of other "fractured fairy tales." In our discussion, I made sure to address point of view and how this perspective influences the telling of a story.

I didn't pre-teach any vocabulary from this story, because I felt the students would be able to read it on their own. I invited predictions about how the story would be different as told from the perspective of the wolf.

To reinforce the strategy of questioning and self-monitoring during reading, I read the first five pages aloud to the students, modeling my own think-alouds as I read:

> Page 1: I'll let you in on a little secret. Nobody knows the real story, because nobody has ever heard my side of the story.

My think-aloud: "People always say there are two sides to every argument. I can't imagine sympathizing with the wolf's side. He's probably going to say that it's just the nature of wolves to eat pigs and wolves have to do what they can to survive."

> Page 4: The real story is about a sneeze and a cup of sugar.

My think-aloud: Don't tell me he's going to tell us that he was just sneezing when he was huffing and puffing. Give me a break! But I wonder about the sugar?

During Reading

When I distributed the books for reading, I gave each student three large sticky notes and asked them to put one at the end of page 13 (when the first pig was eaten), one at the end of page 17 (when the second pig died), and one at the end of the book. I instructed them to write what they are thinking at each point—questions, connections, observations—just as I had modeled. Then I sent them off to read independently.

After Reading

During the next Guided Reading session, we revisited everyone's think-alouds, comparing our ideas and sharing our strategies for correcting points of confusion. Because this was an excellent text for character analysis, we completed a Story Pyramid together. This led to a discussion of whether we really believed the wolf or not, and we revisited the newspaper-like format of the cover. We wrapped up the discussion by rereading the story aloud in partners, and many of the students chose to use this format of retelling a story from another perspective in Writer's Workshop.

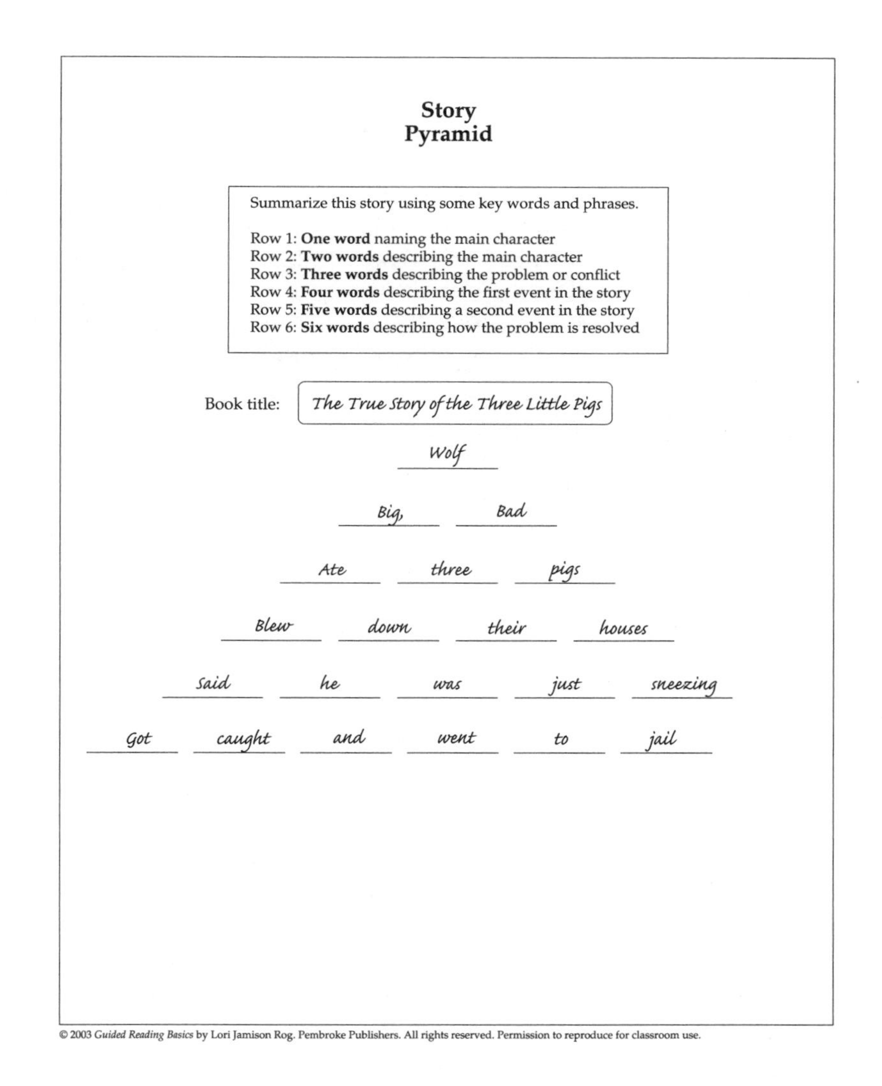

Story Pyramid

Summarize this story using some key words and phrases.

Row 1: **One word** naming the main character
Row 2: **Two words** describing the main character
Row 3: **Three words** describing the problem or conflict
Row 4: **Four words** describing the first event in the story
Row 5: **Five words** describing a second event in the story
Row 6: **Six words** describing how the problem is resolved

Book title: *The True Story of the Three Little Pigs*

Wolf

Big, Bad

Ate three pigs

Blew down their houses

Said he was just sneezing

Got caught and went to jail

Fluent readers are well on their way to becoming independent, strategic learners. As teachers, our most important job is to provide them with texts that scaffold their development, with instruction in building and refining the strategies they have begun to develop, and with a climate that encourages risk and maintains reading engagement.

Story Pyramid

Summarize this story using some key words and phrases.

Row 1: **One word** naming the main character
Row 2: **Two words** describing the main character
Row 3: **Three words** describing the problem or conflict
Row 4: **Four words** describing the first event in the story
Row 5: **Five words** describing a second event in the story
Row 6: **Six words** describing how the problem is resolved

Book title:

10 Phonics Instruction

The threads of letter, sound, and word study should be woven into every fibre of the balanced literacy program. We want our earliest readers to learn how letters represent sounds that may be combined into words. We want our developing readers to apply a variety of strategies in solving unfamiliar words. And we want our fluent readers to understand how to use letter patterns and chunks of meaning to determine both the pronunciation and meaning of new vocabulary. When we provide instruction in letters, sounds, and language concepts within the framework of the Guided Reading lesson, we teach our students that these are not isolated skills, but integral aspects of reading.

Balanced word-study instruction employs a "whole–part–whole" orientation; in other words, as students interact with whole texts, we draw elements of language to study in isolation, then ensure that students have opportunities to apply this learning in context of authentic reading experiences. (Strickland, in *Educational Leadership*, 55:6, March 1998).

Instruction in word study should be part of every component of the literacy program, at all stages of development. During shared book experiences, writing workshops, and interactive read-alouds, we draw students' attention to the way words look and sound. The Guided Reading lesson lends itself ideally to instruction, reinforcement, and application of phonetic concepts in the context of meaningful and connected reading.

Phonics Study in the Guided Reading Lesson

Phonics Study for Emergent Readers

Tip

It is expedient to teach students the names of letters and the sounds they represent at the same time. In fact, 22 of the 26 letter names contain their corresponding sounds.

The first concept emergent readers must develop is the alphabetic principle, and understanding of the relationship between letters and sounds. In a balanced literacy program, children need many opportunities to experiment with how symbols represent ideas in writing as well as in reading.

Research indicates that some traditional practices, such as reciting the alphabet from memory, do not contribute significantly to learning to read (Rog, 2001). Mature readers can identify a letter in isolation and know how it fits into the alphabet, what sound it represents, and how it combines with other letters to form words, but beginning readers cannot. It is far more effective to teach alphabet letters in the context of children's names and other significant words. This enables them to see a purpose for letters and how they fit into the grand scheme of reading. The Name Wall is an excellent tool for teaching and reinforcing alphabet sounds in the context of the children's own names.

Most of the reading your emergent readers do relies on memorization of language patterns and application of high-frequency words. At this stage, we want students to begin to apply letter–sound knowledge to decoding unfamiliar words. Most children will learn to apply beginning consonants (front door sounds) first, followed by ending consonants (back door sounds). Recognition and application of medial vowels and consonants comes later.

The National Reading Panel (2000) has stated that phonics instruction is essential during the first two years of school, and that letter–sound instruction should be provided along with reinforcement of phonemic awareness. As students develop independence in reading, they learn to apply knowledge of the alphabetic principle to the sounds they hear in words.

Phonics Study for Early Readers

Once students have mastered the alphabetic principle, generally at the early-reading level, they have a tendency to over-rely on sounding out as a word-solving strategy. At this stage, we want to encourage readers to use a variety of cueing strategies. We also want to teach them to look for patterns in the way letters go together.

> Tyler is confident in his knowledge of alphabet letters and sounds. But in one early-level text, he was confused by the word "cage." Carefully, he began to sound it out : "*k-a-g-uh*—kagguh?"
>
> Clearly, letter-by-letter decoding was not helping. It would have been much more effective for Tyler to look for a familiar pattern in the word, in this case, the "-age" family.

Rimes are letter chunks consisting of a vowel and the letters that come after it in a syllable. Onsets are the phonemes we attach to rimes to make words.

Word families are also known as *phonograms* or *rimes*, and they are the building blocks of words. Rimes are letter chunks consisting of a vowel and the letters that come after it in a syllable, such as *-ack*, *-ink*, and *-oke*. Not coincidentally, words containing the same rime — for example, "black," "stack," "jack"—rhyme! A classic study by Wylie and Durell (1967) found that only 37 rimes make up almost 500 primary-level words. In their study, they analyzed almost 300 rimes and found that, in 96% of cases, the vowel sound was constant in all words containing that rime. That's certainly a convincing reason to teach and reinforce vowel sounds in the context of word families! Not only that, brain research tells us that the brain looks for patterns in learning. According to Patricia Cunningham (1992), focusing on letter patterns such as rimes and *onsets* (the phonemes we attach to the rimes to make words) supports both reading and spelling.

Phonics Study for Developing and Fluent Readers

Of course, rimes are not the only letter patterns we want our students to know. At the developing- and fluent-reading levels, we want our students to recognize prefixes, suffixes, and root words, and to apply language structures such as plurals, compounds, and contractions to their reading. Explicitly teaching and building lists of common "chunks of meaning" provide our students with important tools for decoding and spelling. For example, we might create lists of prefixes that change the meaning of a root word to mean its opposite, such as *un-*, *dis-*, *mis-*, *in-*. We also need to teach students how adding suffixes such as *-ation* or *-ness* change the meanings and structures of familiar words.

Common Rimes

The following 37 rimes make up over 500 primary-level words:

-ack	-ail	-ain	-ake	-ale	-ame
-an	-ank	-ap	-ash	-at	-ate
-aw	-ay	-eat	-ell	-est	-ice
-ick	-ide	-ight	-ill	-in	-ine
-ing	-ink	-ip	-it	-ock	-oke
-op	-ore	-ot	-uck	-ug	-ump
-unk					

I Can Spell

If I know this word…	*I can read and spell…*		
e.g., black	stack	track	jacket

Word-solving Activities

Tip

Commercial word games like Scrabble, Boggle, Spill and Spell, and Scattergories draw students' attention to creating words and also build vocabulary. You can also design your own word games from traditional games such as Go Fish, Concentration, or Bingo.

Word-study activities generally take place before or after the reading of the text. Before reading, we introduce key words and concepts, drawing attention to language concepts and letter patterns. During reading, we guide each student to apply increasingly flexible word-solving strategies to negotiating unfamiliar words. After reading, we review and reinforce application of strategies, and introduce new letter patterns and structures.

The Name Wall

The Name Wall is a tool for whole-class instruction in the balanced literacy program, but it is also used as a key reference for linking letters and sounds to meaningful words. Each day, one student's name is drawn. This is an important day for that student, who then becomes the leader and special person of the day.

We spell the name out loud, count the letters, and compare the name to those already on the Name Wall. We might build oral language skills by interviewing the leader and recording the information on a chart. With great ceremony, we add the student's name to the appropriate alphabet letter on the wall. We make frequent references to the name wall: "That word starts with a *d*, just like *David*." In this way, we are using the most important words in our students' lives—their names—to reinforce the sounds of the alphabet.

Show What You Know

Show What You Know is a word and letter-concept strategy for our very earliest readers. Hold up the cover of the book they are about to read and ask individuals to come up and "show what you know." Demonstrate how Sara might know the letter *S* in her name, or how Dan might see some letters from his name in the word "and." Some students will know entire words or parts of words. This activity honors each child's language development and extends their thinking about concepts of letters and words.

Chunk Chart

The Chunk Chart is a type of Word Wall that focuses on word families, or rimes. As you study a particular word family, brainstorm a list of words. Have the students vote for the word they want to put on the wall to remind them of that pattern. That word becomes a reference for reading and spelling other words containing this pattern.

> When we read a text about *Snails* in a Guided Reading lesson, we brainstormed a list that included *rail, hail, mail, fail, wail* and *sail.* The students chose the word "snail" to represent this word family on the chunk chart.

The Chunk Chart may be used for games such as Rhyming Word-O and Silly Rhymes.

Rhyming Word-O

Provide each student with a grid of 9, 16, or 25 squares. Students fill in the squares with words from word families, not using the focus words on the Chunk Chart. For example, if the focus word for the* -ing *family is "sing," then students must write in another word, like "bring" or "sting," in one square on their cards.

To play, call out words from the Chunk Chart, as in Bingo. When a word is called, students circle a word they have that rhymes with that word.

Tip

Toy glasses from the dollar store or binoculars made from toilet-paper rolls can be great props for helping readers hunt for letter patterns.

Word Hunts

After reading, send your students to scrounge in their Guided Reading texts or in environmental print around the room for specific language concepts you have studied, such as double letters or words ending in *-s*. Give each student a word framer, a piece of sticky string, or removable highlighting tape to mark a word they have found.

Word Building

Based on the Making Words activity developed by Patricia Cunningham (1992), Word Building is a strategy that involves manipulating letters to create words. Students can see how adding, deleting, or changing one letter can change a word. They learn to look for commonalities and differences in words. They attend explicitly and systematically to the ways in which letters go together.

Choose a vocabulary word or letter pattern you want to reinforce with the students. Using letter tiles, cards, or plastic alphabet letters, provide students with the letters they need to create the focus word. For beginning readers, you will want to provide explicit instruction in manipulating the letters. Keep the lesson short and fast-paced, with only six to ten word changes, depending on the objectives of the lesson. Prepare word cards so that students see each word in its entirety after they have created it with the separate letters.

Word Building can be used as a before- or after-reading strategy. Before reading, it is particularly effective for teaching new vocabulary or strategies at the early-reading level. After reading, it may be used to reinforce language patterns encountered in the reading. Cunningham emphasizes that making words is only the first step in the process, followed by *sorting* the words that have been created, and then *transferring* the knowledge to new situations.

My early-reading group is about to read a book called *All Clean*. The word "clean" is reinforced throughout the book, as "clean," "cleaned," "cleaning," and even "vacuum cleaner." I provide each student with a set of letters: *a, e, e, c, l, n, r*. I guide them to create words with the letters:

1. Take *a* and *n* to create the word "an."
2. Put a *c* at the beginning, and what word do you have? ["can"]
3. add an *e* to the end, and what word do you have? ["cane"]
4. Change the *c* to *l*, and what word do you have? ["lane"]
5. Move the *e* between the *l* and the *a*, and what word do you have? ["lean"]
6. Add the *c* to the beginning of the word, and what word do you have? ["clean"]
7. What word can you make with all the letters? ["cleaner"]
8. What changes would you have to make to create "cleaning" and "cleaned"?

After reading, we revisit the activity to brainstorm words with the *-ean* family and choose one representative word to add the Chunk Chart.

Tip

Inexpensive magnetic letters on metal burner covers are ideal for Word Building activities in Guided Reading groups.

Silly Rhymes

One of the best ways to engage students in purposeful language play and to reinforce rimes and onsets is to have students create Silly Rhymes. They're fun because the students don't have to worry about rhythm or logic. They're effective because they require students to manipulate language for meaning. After brainstorming or reading lists of word-family words, model making a Silly Rhyme, such as "The mean bean was very clean." Students in the Guided Reading group can take turns creating their own Silly Rhymes orally or in writing.

> One group of early readers decided to create their own word- family flip books. They compiled booklets by stapling four short strips of paper on top of two long ones. On the first long strip they wrote a rime, such as *-ick*. On each short strip, they wrote one appropriate onset, such as *st-*, *s-*, *tr-*, and *br-*. On the bottom long strip, they wrote a silly rhyme using at least two of the word-family words —"The magic stick did a funny trick."

Word Ladders

Provide sheets with blank ladders on them (see page 94), and invite students to "climb the ladder" by writing in as many words as they can for each word family. Make it a contest to see who can climb highest on the ladder with correctly spelled word-family words. (Score 10 points for each word and count by tens to total the score.)

I Can Spell

Encourage students to apply what they have learned about word families to decoding and spelling new words. Have them work individually or in groups to fill in an I Can Spell chart (see page 89).

Word-solving Strategies

Our main goal for word study is to provide students with strategies for independence. Fountas and Pinnell (1998) refer to the process of figuring out unfamiliar words as "word solving" because it involves a variety of strategies beyond simply decoding. Here are the top ten tips for word solving:

1. **Checking**—Check the picture to help you figure out the word.
2. **Chunking**—See if you recognize any "chunks" or patterns. Is there a little word inside the big word?
3. **Cross-checking**—Use word walls and other classroom charts as a reference for solving words in text.
4. **Stretching**—Stretch the sounds in the word; sound it out.
5. **Sliding**—Take a running start and slide right into the word
6. **Monitoring**—Stop and think about whether the word makes sense, sounds right, and matches the print.
7. **Skipping**—Skip a hard word and read on; sometimes the rest of the sentence will help you with the word.
8. **Rereading**—Go back to the beginning of the sentence and start again.
9. **Fixing**—If you read a word that doesn't make sense, sound right, or look right, go back and fix it up. That's what good readers do!
10. **Guessing**—Guess what word might make sense in the sentence. See if the sounds in your guess match the letters on the page.

Teach these strategies one at a time, modeling them and providing opportunities for guided practice. Some teachers like to maintain classroom charts to remind students of the strategies they should be using.

Concentration

Make a set of 40 cards, half with rimes and half with onsets. Students place all the cards face down and take turns drawing pairs of cards. If they draw a pair that forms a word, they keep the cards and make another draw. When all the cards are gone, or no longer form words, the person with the most pairs wins.

Create Strategy Bookmarks by cutting and pasting the icons on page 95. Choose three to five strategies that you have studied and that you want the students to focus on. Laminate these bookmarks for the students to use as placemarkers and strategy reminders.

Word Sorts

Word Sorts require the students to group words according to categories, based on criteria ranging from meaning to letter patterns. Sometimes we provide the criteria by which students will sort a group of words; sometimes we will have them establish their own categories.

After a Word Building exercise, we often sort the words we have created according to word family. You might ask students to sort words according to the number of syllables, the vowel sound, or the ending pattern, such as words in which *-ed* adds an extra syllable ("wanted") and words in which it doesn't ("walked").

Sorting requires students to attend to a variety of language concepts in a critical and thoughtful way. When students sort words according to their own categories, they should be required to articulate the system they used.

Word Ladder

100	100	100
90	90	90
80	80	80
70	70	70
60	60	60
50	50	50
40	40	40
30	30	30
20	20	20
10	10	10
Word Family: ____________________	Word Family: ____________________	Word Family: ____________________

Icons for Strategy Bookmarks

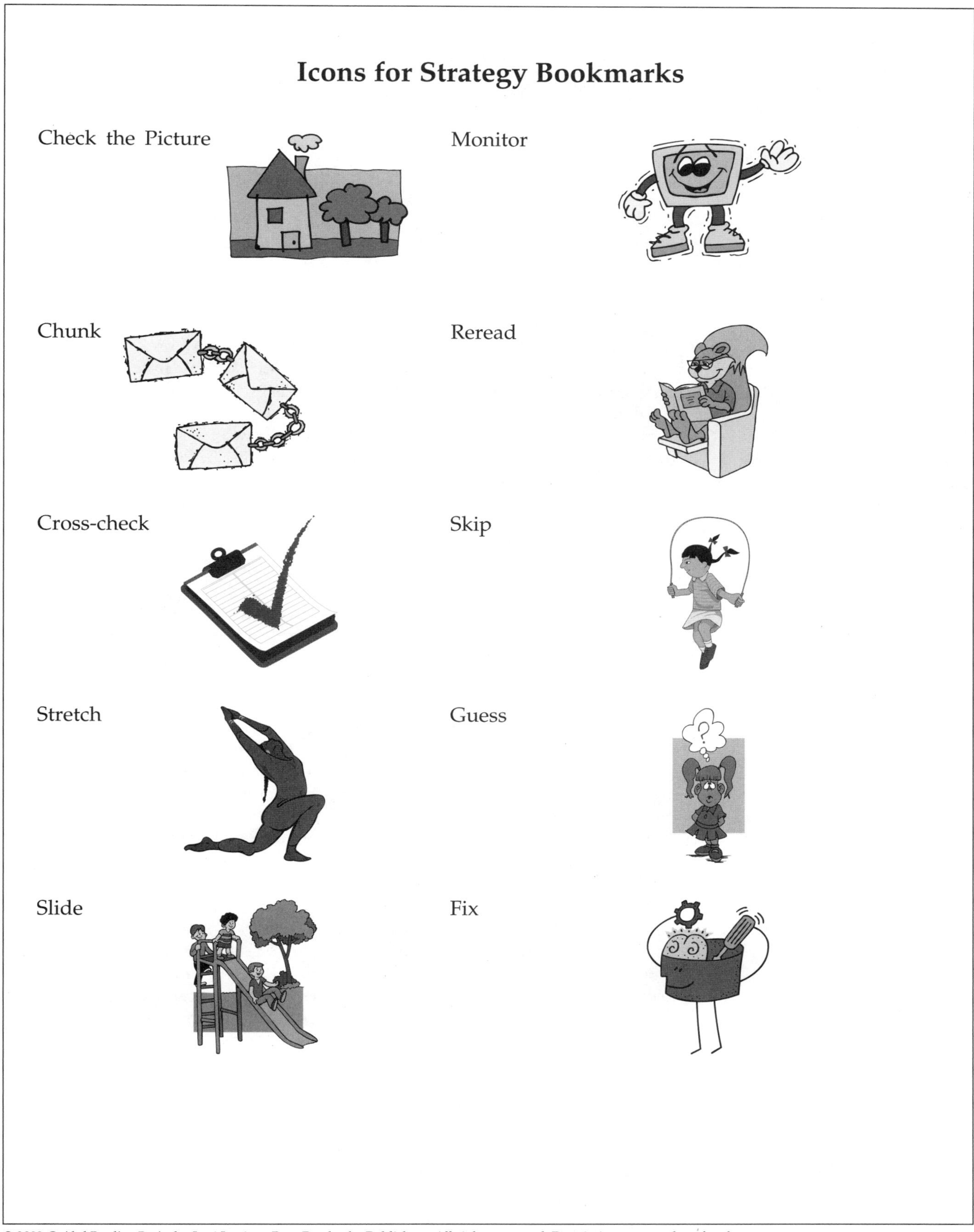

11 Vocabulary and High-Frequency Word Study

Did you know that 100 basic words account for half of all the reading we do in English? No wonder they're called high-frequency words! Words like "what," "of," "the," and "to" are like the glue that holds most of our text together; however, they are often not decodable, and they do not carry meaning in themselves. That's why we sometimes call these *sight words;* we want readers to recognize them instantly, to increase fluency and enhance comprehension.

High-frequency words are the basic words that join and hold text together. They are also called anchor words and sight words.

High-frequency words are one component of word study in the Guided Reading program; the other is vocabulary instruction. While half of all the words we read are high-frequency words, the other half of our reading includes some half million words in the English language. Vocabulary is one of those issues that seemed to have fallen victim to that old educational pendulum, which swung from pre-teaching virtually every word the students might possibly encounter to abandoning pre-teaching totally with the belief that students would solve words from context. Today, research reminds us that balance is in order (National Reading Panel, 2000). Some words must be pre-taught in order to ensure that readers understand the text; others should be left to the reader's own cueing strategies.

Reading Fluency

It is important for readers at all levels to develop a cadre of high-frequency words that they recognize at sight. The ability to recognize many words automatically is an essential element of fluency, which has been closely linked to comprehension at all levels (National Reading Panel, 2000). Fluency refers to the ability to read quickly, accurately, and with appropriate intonation. Nonfluent readers devote so much effort and energy to decoding individual words that they essentially have no working memory left to devote to comprehension. Also, when readers read slowly, they do not read as much. Word by word decoding "slows down the [reading] process and takes up valuable resources that are necessary for comprehension." (National Reading Panel, 2000, pp. 3–8).

At emergent and early reading levels, sentences and texts are short enough that word-by-word reading doesn't interfere with comprehension. As sentences become longer and more complex, however, dysfluent reading impedes comprehension. At the developing reading level, it is important that students learn to read quickly and efficiently in meaningful phrases.

Nonfluent readers are more likely to...	Fluent readers are more likely to...
...read hesitantly, word by word.	...read with speed, expression, and phrasing.
...sound out words letter by letter.	...decode words by patterns and chunks.
...use phonics as their only cueing strategy.	...flexibly use a variety of strategies.
...be interrupted whenever they make a miscue.	...be expected to self-correct.
...rely on the teacher to prompt.	...monitor their own comprehension.
...read on even if it doesn't make sense.	...go back to reread and cross-check.

There are a number of things teachers can do to promote reading fluency:

- Ensure that students have reading materials that are not too difficult for them; even skilful readers lack fluency when reading texts with too many unfamiliar words.
- Help students develop a repertoire of cueing strategies; dysfluent reading often results from over-reliance on sounding out every word.
- Take care with our own responses while students are reading; when we intervene too frequently, we train our students to be hesitant as they read.
- Model fluent reading in shared reading and read-aloud experiences.

Fluency is important. But it is a means toward increased reading proficiency, not an end in itself. The primary emphasis in reading instruction is comprehension; however, when students can read with fluency, they are likely to read more, read better, and enjoy it more.

Vocabulary Instruction

In addition to reinforcing high-frequency words, it is also important for readers to increase their vocabulary and their abilities to negotiate unfamiliar words. We want our students to understand how the language of books can paint pictures in their minds and evoke emotions in their souls.

Some aspects of word study are most effectively taught to a large group, then reinforced with individuals or small groups as needed within the Guided Reading setting. High-frequency words and other Word Wall activities, specialized vocabulary for a science or social studies theme, letter patterns, and spelling strategies may be most efficiently presented as whole-class instruction.

The Guided Reading lesson then becomes the vehicle for applying this knowledge to text before, during, and after reading. Before reading, we introduce selected vocabulary words that will be essential to understanding of the text. During reading, we scaffold students as they apply word-solving strategies with increasing independence. After reading, we review, reinforce, and extend vocabulary and concept knowledge.

Tip

The best strategy for increasing students' vocabulary is plenty of reading.

Much vocabulary knowledge is acquired automatically by reading; the more you read, the more your vocabulary grows. As teachers, we also want to provide explicit instruction in the relationships between words and concepts, and to help our students develop an interest in words and language. Research has shown that the least effective way to teach vocabulary is by learning definitions (Allen, 1999).

Fountas and Pinnell (1998, p. 166) suggest the following principles for effective vocabulary instruction:

- New words should be integrated with familiar words and concepts.
- Students should experience words in repeated, meaningful encounters.
- Students should apply the words they learn to other contexts and in other associations.
- Instruction should actively engage students in processing word meanings.

When we have an interest in how language goes together, we are more likely to pay attention to words and increase our vocabularies. Bulletin boards that display collections of "million-dollar words" (words and phrases that capture our attention) stimulate an interest in vocabulary. Word games and puzzles build spelling skills and strengthen vocabulary. Words that come from other languages such as the German "kindergarten" or Spanish "mosquito," portmanteau words such as "brunch," and words from people's names such as "sandwich" can also prove fascinating to young readers.

Word Study in the Guided Reading Lesson

Word Study for Emergent and Early Readers

Because emergent readers rely on memorizing patterns and pictures to negotiate texts, they are unable to "read" words they don't know. In addition to developing their speaking vocabularies, we also want to begin to build a repertoire of words they recognize at sight, words like "to," "for," "here," and "is."

> My emergent-level reading group is about to read a story entitled "Dear Santa." The repeated sentence in the book is "Dear Santa, Thank you for the...," with a different concept word each time. Although they memorize this pattern quite easily, I want to make sure they can isolate and identify those high-frequency words: "you," "for," and "the." "The" is already on the Word Wall and the students pick it out easily. We spell each word out loud, snapping our fingers, and sing the spelling to the tune of "Hot Cross Buns." I open the book and invite students to frame any of our focus words.

Early readers encounter mostly high-frequency and decodable words in their reading. As they learn to apply letter–sound correspondences to solving words, many students begin to sound out every word they read! They need to build their collection of sight words as well as learning flexible cueing strategies.

Word Study for Developing and Fluent Readers

The need to extend and build a student's vocabulary of high-frequency words does not end at emergent and early reading stages. Reading fluency has been strongly linked to comprehension at higher levels (National Reading Panel, 2000). Fluent readers recognize many words instantly; however, the more words a reader must decode, the less fluent his reading will be. Equally important is the need to continually increase each reader's personal vocabulary and ability to access increasingly complex words and concepts.

Fluent-level text is characterized by literary language and longer and more complex sentences. As teachers, we need to make informed choices about which words to pre-teach and what strategies our students need to be able to access the rest of the vocabulary independently. Our decisions about which vocabulary words to pre-teach, should be based on the answers to these questions:

- Is the word crucial to students' understanding and appreciation of the text?
- Will students be able to solve it on their own from context?
- Is a superficial exposure to the word adequate or is deep understanding needed?

Word Study Activities

Word Study activities will generally take place before or after the reading of the text. Before reading, we introduce anchor words and unique vocabulary. During reading, we want the students to apply their sight-word knowledge and word-solving strategies to negotiation of the text. Our role as teachers during this time is always to scaffold each reader and provide support as needed. After reading, we review and extend vocabulary knowledge, and reinforce word-solving strategies.

High-Frequency Word Walls

Word Wall instruction is generally presented to the whole class, but the words on the Wall are then reviewed and reinforced as needed within the Guided Reading lesson.

Word Walls are one of the most effective tools for teaching and reinforcing high-frequency words. A Word Wall is more than a display of words. It is an approach to teaching that involves

- "harvesting" featured words from actual reading and writing experiences
- explicitly teaching the words using a variety of learning modes —visual, auditory, and kinesthetic
- application of language concepts to other reading and writing situations

Remember that there is a difference between having a Word Wall and using or doing a Word Wall! Words on the wall must have meaning and purpose for the students. They should be drawn from authentic reading, explicitly taught, and explicitly transferred to other learning situations. Shared book experiences, group poems, classroom read-alouds, and Guided Reading texts are all sources of high-frequency words. Putting a word on the Word Wall is also an excellent way to pre-teach anchor words that a Guided Reading group is likely to encounter in future reading. It is this purposeful teaching that distinguishes a Word Wall from a word bank of theme words pertinent to a particular unit of study.

INTRODUCING WORD-WALL WORDS

One of the keys to internalizing the words on the Word Wall is to make sure they are overlearned, using a variety of learning modes, such as visual, auditory, and kinesthetic. Before adding a new word to the Word Wall,

Fry's 300 Instant Sight Words

First Hundred

a
about
after
again
all
an
and
any
are
as
at
be
been
before
boy
but
by
can
come
day
did
do
down
eat
for
from
get
give
go
good
had
has
have
he
her
his
him
his
how
I
if
in
is
it
just
know
like
little
long
make
man
many
me
much
my
new
no
not
of
old
on
one
or
other
our
out
put
said
see
she
so
some
take
that
the
their
them
then
there
they
this
three
to
two
up
us
very
was
we
were
what
when
which
who
will
with
work
would
you
your

Second Hundred

also
am
another
away
back
ball
because
best
better
big
black
book
both
box
bring
call
came
color
could
dear
each
ear
end
far
find
first
five
found
four
friend
girl
got
hand
high
home
house
into
kind
last
leave
left
let
live
look
made
may
men
more
morning
most
mother
must
name
near
never
next
night
only
open
over
own
people
play
please
present
pretty
ran
read
red
right
run
saw
say
school
seem
shall
should
soon
stand
such
sure
tell
than
these
thing
think
too
tree
under
until
upon
use
want
way
where
while
white
wish
why
year

Third Hundred

along
always
anything
around
ask
ate
bed
brown
buy
car
carry
clean
close
clothes
coat
cold
cut
didn't
does
dog
don't
door
dress
early
eight
every
eyes
face
fall
fast
fat
fine
fire
fly
food
full
funny
gave
goes
green
grow
hat
happy
hard
head
hear
help
hold
hope
hot
jump
keep
letter
longer
love
might
money
myself
now
o'clock
offonce
order
pair
part
ride
round
same
sat
second
set
seven
show
sing
sister
sit
six
sleep
small
start
stop
ten
thank
third
those
though
today
took
town
try
turn
walk
warm
wash
water
woman
write
yellow
yes
yesterday

- see and say the word
- spell and count the letters
- chant or cheer the letters in the word
- pantomime or use actions with the spelling of the word
- make connections to words already known
- print the word
- find the correct spot on the wall for the word

The Word Wall strategy is a quick and effective method of teaching and reinforcing high-frequency words as well as letter patterns. It is important to pull these words from familiar texts, and it is just as important to put the word back in the context of reading-connected text. Send the students on a word hunt to find the featured word in environmental print in the classroom or in a book. Take advantage of many opportunities to reinforce the words on the wall during Guided Reading and independent learning activities.

For today's reading, my early reading group is going to need the words "why" and "how," so I have decided to bring all the students together for a Word Wall lesson on these words. I start by printing the word "why" on a bright pink card. (Using different colors provides another clue to help students remember the words.) Together we look at the word, say the word together and count the letters. We talk about how many sounds we hear in the word compared to how many letters, and if the *h* is silent or if it makes us say the *w* sound in a little different way. This problem-solving discussion helps students attend to the sound of the word.

Sunir suggests that we "body spell" the word, a favorite activity with all the students. They stand up and spell the word letter by letter, raising their hands in the air for tall letters like the *h*, putting their hands on their hips for short letters like the *w*, and touching their toes for letters with tails like the *y*. The physical activity adds another mode of learning to reinforce the spelling.

We look at the Word Wall to see if this word reminds us of any we already know. Some students read other three-letter words. Holly points out that her name ends with the same letter as "why." This is a good opportunity to point out that sometimes *y* makes the long-*i* sound and sometimes it makes the long-*e* sound. We notice that one of our Word Wall words—"what"—also begins with *wh-*. Students get additional reinforcement—as well practice in letter formation—by printing the word on their mini slates. Finally, we post the word in its alphabetic spot on the Word Wall. The whole lesson takes about five minutes.

Introducing High-Frequency Words

Marie Clay suggests that we pre-teach high frequency "anchor words" that students will encounter in their Guided Reading text. If you are introducing a word that is not yet on the classroom Word Wall, use a multi-modal approach to see, say, write, and pantomime the spelling of the word, just as you would with the Word Wall. Some ideas for introducing high-frequency words include

1. **Body Spelling**—Stretch hands in the air as you say tall letters (letters with ascenders), put hands on hips as you say short letters, and touch toes as you say tail letters (letters with descenders).

2. **Fireworks**—Start from a crouched position and gradually stretch upward as you say each letter, finally "exploding" with a leap into the air as you say the whole word.
3. **Different Styles**—Say each letter in a whisper, with noses plugged, in a squeaky voice, etc.
4. **Rhythm**—Spell the word in a rhythm with a clap or snap between each letter. Invite different students to create the rhythm
5. **Singing**—Sing the letters to a familiar melody, such as "Hot Cross Buns" for three-letter words or "This Land is Your Land" for five-letter words.
6. **Tracing**—Trace the letters in the air or on the next person's back
7. **Printing Practice**—Print the words on paper, or on individual white boards, magnetic boards, or "magic slates."
8. **Marshmallow Clap**—Almost clap, but stop before your hands touch. At the end of the spelling, say the word as you *smoosh* the imaginary marshmallow with your hands and pop it into your mouth.
9. **Graphing**—Graph the word on a chart with each letter of the alphabet.
10. **Word Wall**—Add the word to the classroom Word Wall.

Mind Reader

If an important anchor word is already on the classroom Word Wall, you might draw students' attention to it by playing Mind Reader. Tell the students that you are thinking of a word on the Wall and they have to read your mind to see what it is. Each student numbers a piece of paper from 1 to 5. Give them five clues, and after each clue they must write one guess from the Word Wall. They can write the same word more than once if they are confident it meets the clues, but they must write a word beside each number. The clues start off very general and become so specific that all students can guess the correct word.

> When playing Mind Reader, I gave my students the following clues for the word "what."
>
> Clue #1: It's a word on the Word Wall.
> Clue #2: It has one syllable.
> Clue #3: It has four letters.
> Clue #4: It starts with "w."
> Clue #5: It contains the little word "hat."
>
> This activity forces students to pay attention to many language concepts, and is an effective way to reinforce words on the Word Wall.

Word Wall Yahtzee

This game involves rolling a die, but instead of numbers, the players write words from the high-frequency Word Wall on their score cards (see BLM on page 104). The scoring may be as follows:

If a player rolls a number he has already filled in on his score card, he must choose one empty row to "scratch." The player with the most points at the end wins.

Bang!

This game requires a set of cards showing high-frequency words you have studied, along with four or five cards labeled *Bang!* Students take turns drawing cards and reading the word on the card. If the student can read the word, he or she keeps the word card. A student who draws the Bang! card must return all the word cards he or she has collected, and the game continues until all the word cards are gone.

Tip

Search the party-favors section of a discount or dollar store for magnifying glasses, tracing tools, bubble wands, and other toys to use as word framers. Toy glasses or binoculars also help young readers hunt for words.

Word Hunts

After reading, send your students to scrounge in their Guided Reading texts or in environmental print around the room for specific high-frequency words you have studied. Give each student a word framer, a piece of "sticky string," or removable highlighting tape to mark the word they have found. You can assign students to find particular words, or make it a game by having them draw a word from the high-frequency word card deck.

Building Reading Fluency

The Guided Reading lesson is a perfect opportunity to provide oral reading practice with appropriate level texts, but not to revisit questionable practices such as round-robin reading. Students should always have a chance to practise and engage with a text before being required to read it to an audience. Here are some activities that help build reading fluency:

1. **Unison or choral reading**—When students read together, especially with an experienced reader such as the teacher, all readers join in fluency and expression.
2. **Echo reading**—This involves reading a phrase aloud and having students repeat it.
3. **Phrasing practice**—Work with the students to break up a chunk of two or three sentences into meaningful phrases. Read each phrase aloud and discuss which phrase groupings are most meaningful.
4. **Guided repeated oral reading**—This strategy involves having a student read a passage aloud, receive feedback on the reading, then reread the same passage.
5. **Performance Reading**—Readers theatre and role drama are just two forms of performance reading. Fluency and expression are developed and reinforced when students have the opportunity to practise reading for performance.

Sorting and Categorizing

Chapter 14, on using non-fiction in the Guided Reading program, discusses categorizing to access background knowledge and predict what a text will be about.

Word Sorts require the students to group words according to categories, sometimes pre-determined and sometimes of their own choosing.

Provide each group of students with a set of cards with key words from the story. Have them work together to sort the words into whatever categories they choose, then invite them to predict what the story or information piece will be about, based on the vocabulary presented. Discuss the activity later to ensure that all words are clarified and that students can articulate their rationale for grouping.

Word Wall Yahtzee Score Card

If you roll a...	*Write any word from the word wall that has...*	*Points...*
1	One syllable	1
2	Two syllables	2
3	Three letters	3
4	Four letters	4
5	Five letters	5
6	Six or more letters	6

In a text about animal mothers and babies, I might give the students the following set of word cards to sort and categorize. Then we would discuss the different kinds of groupings they created.			
cow	foal	sheep	horse
cat	calf	gosling	kid
lamb	goat	kitten	goose

Possible Sentences

Students are given words and asked to create sentences that might appear in the story using these words. For example, from the words "beanstalk," "magic," and "giant," students might create this sentence: "The giant climbed up the magic beanstalk." When students work in pairs, they learn from one another.

Collecting Words

In addition to teaching our students new words, we also want them to build their own vocabularies by attending to the words they read. Shelly Galloway, a Grade 2 teacher, keeps a permanent bulletin board of "million-dollar words" and encourages her students to add words and phrases that capture their attention. As part of a theme study, info-text reading, or even response to a narrative, you can have the students work in groups or as a class to develop a word bank. Using the Alphabet Chart graphic organizer on page 106, have them fill as many boxes as they can with words or phrases from or about the story.

"Million-dollar words" are words and phrases that capture our attention.

Context Clues

Many students need to be explicitly taught how to use the context of the passage to help them determine the meaning of unfamiliar vocabulary. Pull passages from Guided Reading texts and talk about how the words and ideas give clues to the meaning of difficult words. Teach students to look for "signal words" that give clues to meaning (see page 146 in Chapter 14).

Word Solving

As readers mature, they develop the ability to decode many words that they don't necessarily understand. Effective readers use a combination of word-solving strategies to solve difficult words.

Model and practise routines, such as these:

- Try to pronounce the word. Does the sound of it help you understand what it means?
- Does this word remind you of any words you already know?
- Are there any prefixes, suffixes, or root words you recognize?
- What clues are in the context of the passage?
- If all else fails, look it up in the dictionary.

Vocabulary-Concept Map

Connecting concepts and labels is an important way to clarify both vocabulary and ideas. For example, "migration" is the label (or name) for the concept of birds traveling to warmer climates during the winter months. Students can clarify concepts by completing a concept map organizer (see BLMs on pages 107 and 108) to zero in on the target word.

Alphabet Chart

A	B	C	D	E
F	G	H	I	J
K	L	M	N	O
P	Q	R	S	T
U	V	W	X,Y	Z

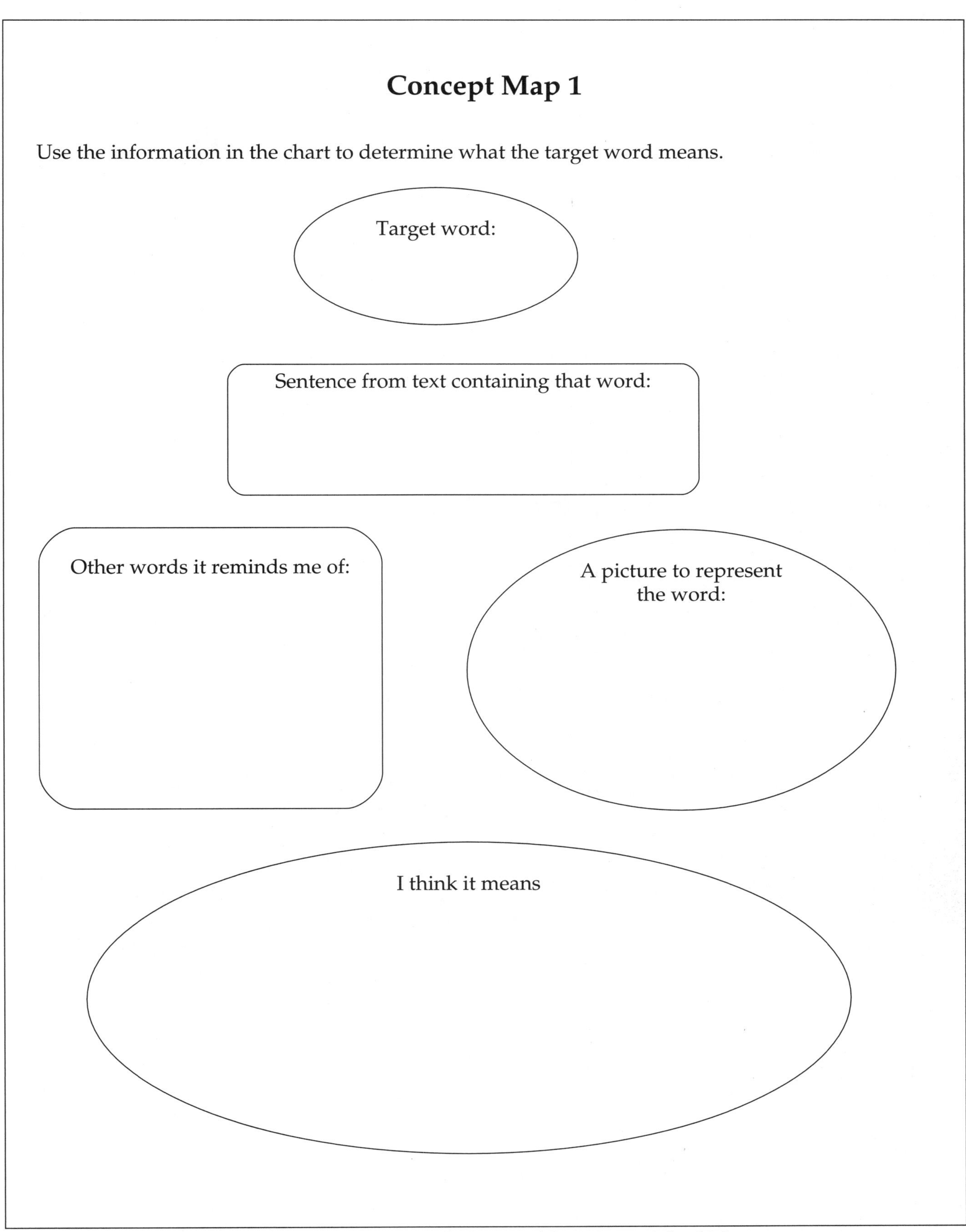
Concept Map 1
Use the information in the chart to determine what the target word means.
Target word:
Sentence from text containing that word:
Other words it reminds me of:
A picture to represent the word:
I think it means

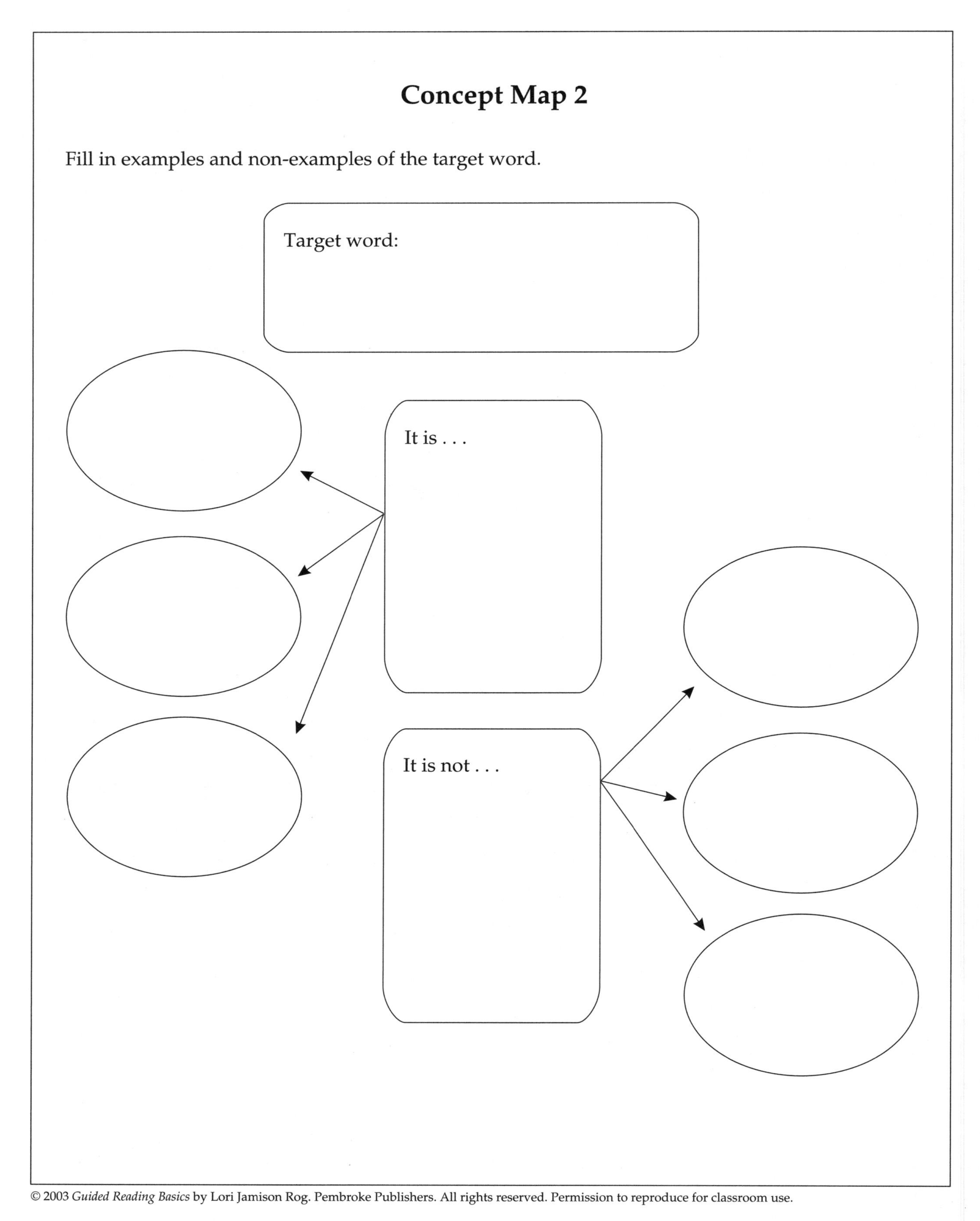

Concept Map 2

Fill in examples and non-examples of the target word.

12 Comprehension Strategies

My daughter Jennifer was a fairly precocious reader. At a young age, she could decode many words that she didn't really understand. On one occasion, she made a particularly egregious miscue and I asked her, "Jennifer, does that make sense to you?" She looked at me incredulously and replied, "You mean it's all supposed to make sense?"

Why do we read? We read to get meaning from print. We read to learn about the world around us. We read to make sense of our own world.

At the emergent level, readers make meaning from texts using pictures and patterns. By the early level, readers are beginning to decode, and sounding out words may take precedence over meaning. Texts for early readers begin to have story lines for readers to understand and recall. This is why retelling is a key strategy for early readers; it will build the foundations for inference and higher-level comprehension later.

Developing and fluent readers devote less energy to word solving and more to comprehension than at earlier levels. Texts at these levels have increasingly complex concepts with many characters and events. Comprehension instruction is vital in order to extend the strategic independence of these readers.

Teaching students to comprehend what they read is a primary goal of the Guided Reading program. But even the most sophisticated reader encounters challenging text at one time or another. What sets the effective reader apart from the ineffective reader is the ability to recognize points of confusion and apply a variety of strategies to correct them. Often struggling readers do not even know that they don't comprehend. And, if they do realize their lack of comprehension, they don't know what to do to fix it. Our ultimate goal is for our students to be strategic, independent readers who monitor their own understanding and know what to do when comprehension fails.

When we teach comprehension strategies, we must also teach students how to recognize when they don't understand, and what to do to correct the misunderstanding. Self-monitoring and fix-up strategies are two essential tools in the comprehension toolbox. They require that the reader not only think about the text, but also think about his or her thinking; in other words, to be metacognitive.

Effective readers use many tools for comprehension and metacognition. They know how to make connections from their existing knowledge and experience to new information that they read. They create mental images to clarify and recall information from text. Most important, perhaps, is that they know how to make inferences and interpretations in order to read beyond the print.

Accessing Prior Knowledge and Making Connections

We all learn new information best when we can connect it to information that we already know. *Schema* are the knowledge and ideas we have in our heads. When new ideas are introduced to us, we *assimilate* them into our existing knowledge bank. Sometimes new knowledge contradicts or corrects what we previously believed, so we have to adjust our existing knowledge bank to *accommodate* it.

Reader Response Theory (Rosenblatt, 1978) teaches us that reading is a transaction between a reader and a text, that each reader brings new meaning to a text based on his or her own previous knowledge and experiences. Teaching students to access this background information and connect it to what they read helps them to understand what they read and make it relevant to their own lives and learning.

In *Mosaic of Thought*, Susan Zimmerman and Ellin Keene suggest that there are three types of connections: *text-to-self*, *text-to-text*, and *text-to-world*. When we read, we sometimes make connections to our own experiences. Sometimes we make connections to something else we have read. And sometimes, we make connections to what we know about important issues in the world, such as friendship, racism, or caring for the environment. (See poster on page 111.)

Effective readers make connections...

Before reading to

- *access prior knowledge*
- *set purpose for reading*
- *establish context*

During reading to

- *understand new information by connecting it to existing knowledge*
- *monitor comprehension by distinguishing new information from what is already known*

After reading to

- *assimilate new information into existing schema*
- *synthesize learning*

Good readers make connections before, during, and after reading. Before reading, inviting students to access prior knowledge is an important component of the book introduction, as it helps to establish a context for reading. During reading, readers are constantly using what they already know to help them understand new information in the text. After reading, readers make connections to synthesize new learning and assimilate it into their knowledge banks. We must teach our students first to make connections, then to know how to use these connections to help them understand what they read.

Text-to-Self Connections

Making personal connections is a comprehension strategy that even the youngest students can develop. Right from emergent stages, we should be asking students "Have you ever...?" or "What does the story remind you of?" Linking reading to personal experiences and knowledge should be a component of every lesson.

As part of the book introduction at emergent and early levels, we ask students to make personal connections to the title and topic by asking questions like, "Have you ever become lost when you went shopping with Mom and Dad?" or "Tell about a time when you went to a birthday party." Students also need to learn that not all connections help them with the reading; sometimes we must guide our students' connections and teach them how these connections help them understand what they read.

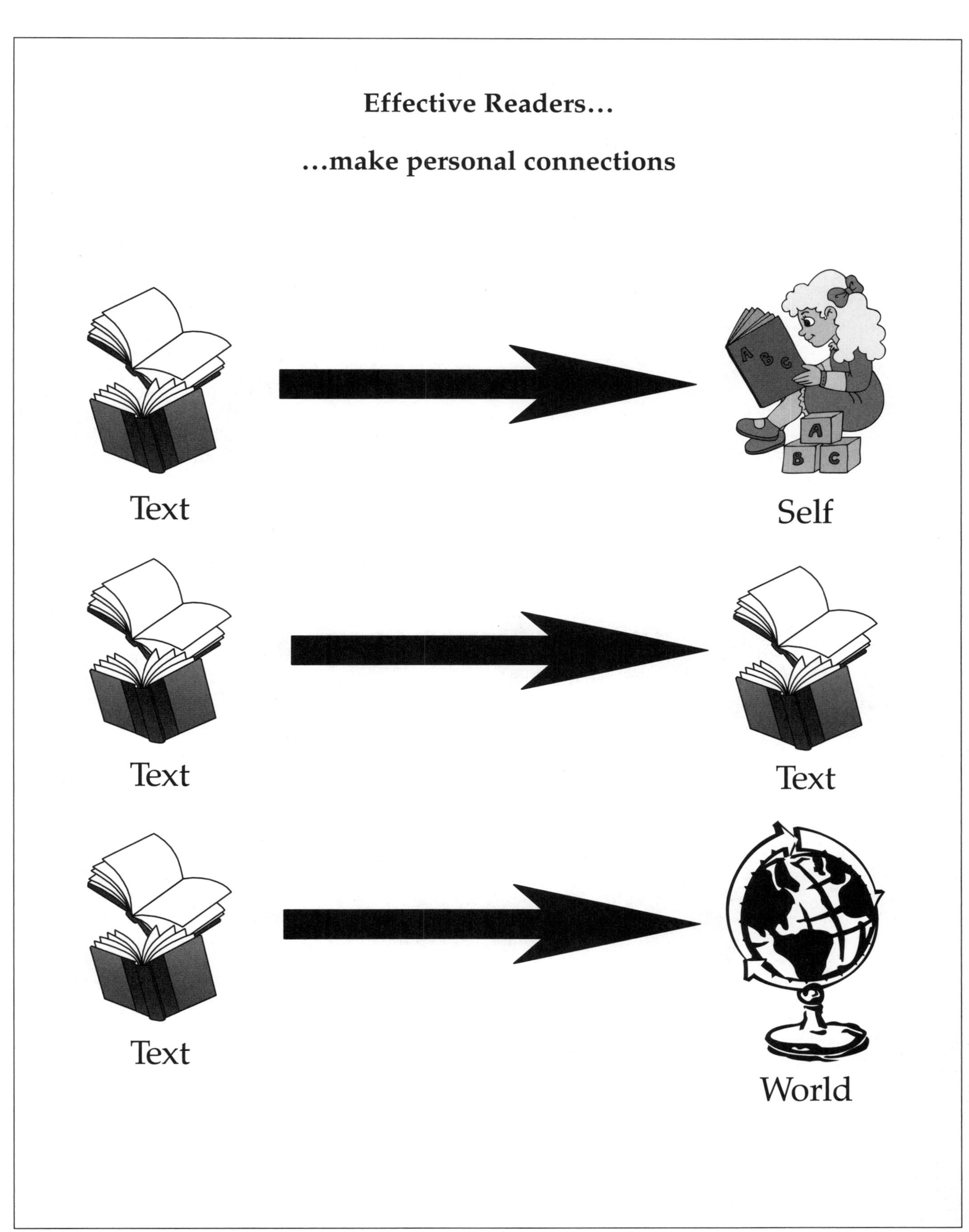
Effective Readers...
...make personal connections
A
B
C
A
B
C
Text
Self
Text
Text
Text
World

One of my favorite texts for teaching emergent readers is *A Sun, A Flower* by Sally Odgers, illustrated by Geoffrey Cox (Wright Group Publishing, 1997), a book about compound words. On the cover is the title and a picture of a big sunflower. If I simply invite connections about the title and the cover, I get observations like "My grandma has sunflowers in her garden" or "My brother likes to spit sunflower seeds at me." If I want the students to make connections that help them understand the text, I need to say, "This is a book about putting two little words together to make a big word, like putting 'sun' and 'flower' together to make 'sunflower,' or putting 'mail' and 'box' together to make 'mailbox.' Can you think of any other little words we can put together to make one big word?" In this way, I am guiding them to make meaningful connections for this particular reading challenge.

Author and teacher Debbie Miller talks to her first graders about using their schema to make connections. She records the connections the students make as they listen to or read a story. After reading, she talks about which connections helped them understand the text and which did not. In this way, she is not only teaching her beginning readers how making connections can be an effective reading strategy, but also how to be metacognitive and think about their thinking as they read.

Text-to-Text Connections

The next level of application is relating text to text. Making connections from one reading experience to another aids comprehension and facilitates understanding and appreciation of literary elements. Some text-to-text connections might include comparing

- different books by the same author
- books on the same theme or topic
- characters
- plots or conflicts
- genre or story structure
- different versions of the same story

Graphic organizers can be used to record text-to-text connections. Venn diagrams (see BLM on pp. 113) are one form of graphic organizer for recording similarities and differences among texts. Unique characteristics of each text are recorded in each of the circles, with common characteristics noted in the overlapping portion of the circles. Another way to compare different books is with a chart, such as the one on page 115.

Text-to-World Connections

One of the most important things reading does is help us learn about the world around us. In our classrooms, we use literature to connect to all kinds of important themes: families, friendship, war, cultures, and courage are just a few. Teaching students to explicitly make text-to-world connections helps to inform them about important issues, to clarify ideas and perspectives, and to teach them to respect individual differences. They develop critical reading skills and learn how reading can make a difference in their lives.

Venn Diagrams

Write things you know about each text in its circle. Write things that are true about both in the place where the circles overlap.

Title: ______________________________ Title: ________________________

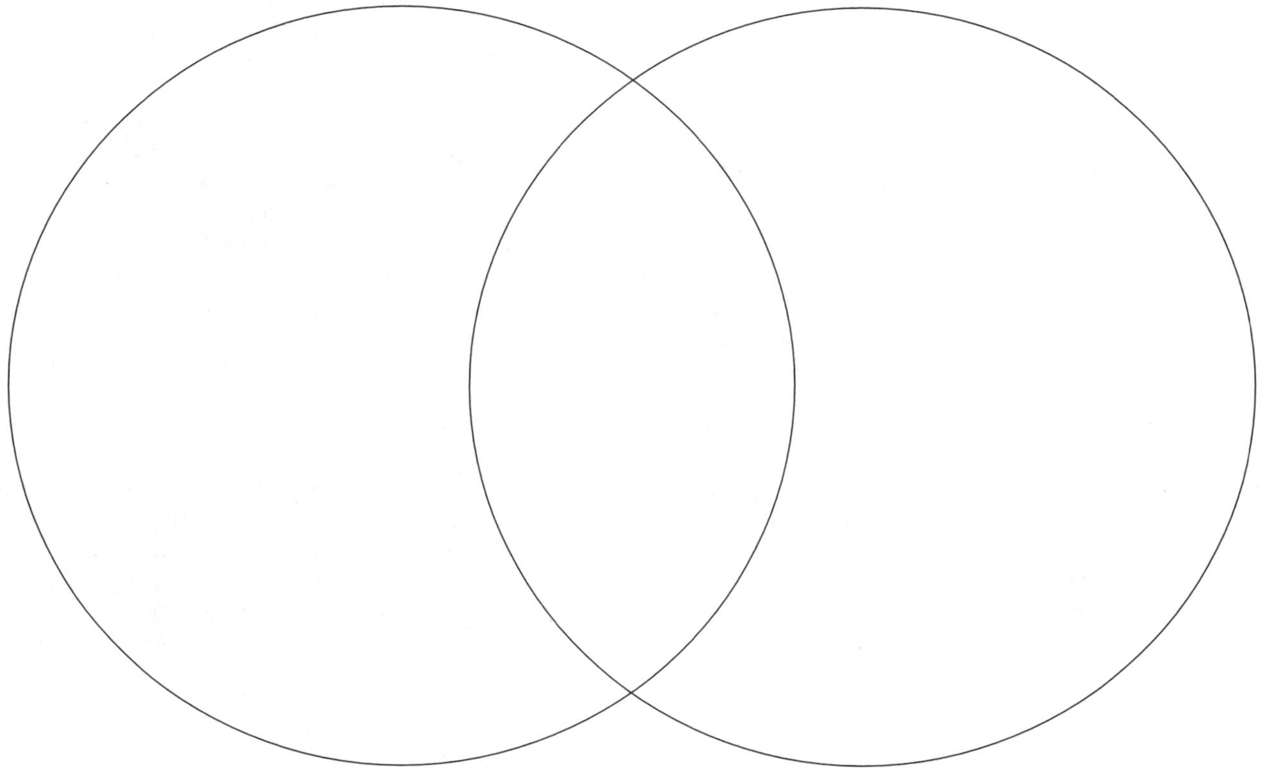

Tip

One way to encourage connections during reading is to have students code their connections on sticky notes. As they read, have them tab points in the text that evoke connections, coding them with T–S for Text-to-Self, T–T for Text-to-Text, and T–W for Text-to-World.

As part of our Guided Reading instruction, we often guide students to make connections before reading to establish a context and purpose. We also want them to make connections as they read, as a way of continually making meaning from text.

After reading, we guide students to make connections to synthesize and consolidate information. Students should be encouraged to write about their connections in their response journals, or to discuss them with a partner or with the group. Extend thinking and make it metacognitive by having students talk about how these connections helped them read.

Coding for Comprehension

As we mentioned at the beginning of this chapter, all readers occasionally struggle with comprehension as they read. Sometimes the vocabulary is too complex, or the reader just doesn't have the necessary prior knowledge to understand the concepts. It's important to teach developing readers first to recognize whether or not they are comprehending, and then to use reading strategies to help them correct the confusion.

The books I read for my book club are quite a bit more complex than the ones I have beside my bed to lull me to sleep. In my book-club books, I always encounter parts that I have a strong connection with, parts that frustrate me, parts with wonderful language, and parts that I don't really understand. I keep a supply of sticky notes on hand to keep track of these "stop and think" points. When I come to the book-club meetings, my books are full of tabs with question marks, stars, and exclamation points. I don't want to interrupt my reading to write long missives about my reactions and confusions, so I just make brief notes, full of codes and abbreviations as reminders.

We need to teach students the same habits of thinking about their reading as well as about the text. They, too, can learn to code their reading responses, and revisit them later or bring them to the group for discussion.

Tip

Cut 3" x 5" sticky notes into "fringes" for students to tear off and use for coding and tabbing.

Throughout this book, I have suggested using sticky notes to mark texts for a variety of purposes. We have looked at coding text-to-self, text-to-text and text-to-world connections. In Chapter 14, I make the suggestion that students may code the information in non-fiction texts with a check mark for facts they already knew, a star for facts they learned, and an exclamation point for amazing facts. In doing this, readers are encouraged to pay attention to new information and connect to existing schema.

VIP Code

Students may be asked to code main ideas in the text, or Very Important Points, with the letters *VIP* (Hoyt, 2002).

We've all taught students who retell stories almost verbatim, from "once upon a time" to "happily ever after." They have a strong literal comprehension of the text, and good memory of events. But they treat every event and detail with equal importance; they seem unable to separate the main ideas from supporting details.

Give such students four sticky notes to use as they read. Each time they encounter an idea that they think is a Very Important Point, they mark it with a VIP tab. If they use up their four sticky notes before completing the reading, they will have to make some choices about which tab to move to another Very Important Point.

After reading, you may want to extend this activity by encouraging reading partners to combine their VIPs and come to a consensus on four points between

Comparison Chart

	Characters	*Problem*	*Solution*
Story A			
Story B			
Story C			

them. This forces them not only to identify the main ideas in the story, but also to justify the choices.

"I Wonder..." Code

One of the simplest and most effective codes is the *?* (question mark) code, which means "I wonder..." Even adult readers wonder about some things when they read. Good writers want to keep us guessing! As Harvey and Goudvis say, "Writers don't spill their thoughts on the page, they leak them slowly, one idea at a time, until the reader can make an educated guess or an appropriate inference about an underlying theme in the text or a prediction about what is to come." (2001, page 23) Using a Big Book or other enlarged text, model and think aloud as you read a text and wonder about some parts. Then you can show your students how, sometimes, you figure out your I Wonder and can go back and remove the *?* or put a check mark over it.

At the end of the reading, have students go back and revisit their I Wonder tabs. The coded notes may also be used to focus a literature circle discussion or guide a personal journal response. It is also important to talk about whether students corrected their misunderstanding, and, if so, what strategies they used.

Color Code

Tip

Keep a classroom chart of fix-it strategies to repair comprehension breaks (see page 119).

The Hot Spots strategy (Hoyt, 2000) involves providing students with red and green flags. When a reader comes to a part of the text that is unclear to them or that they wonder about, they red flag it to stop and pay attention. If they are able to clear up the confusion or if the text subsequently provides an answer, they replace the red flag with a green flag. At the end of the reading, students discuss the strategies they used to correct confusing points, as well as questions from the reading that still remain unanswered.

Three-level Questioning

Many of our students beyond primary levels can decode easily and even comprehend literally, but struggle when the text requires inference and interpretation. An inference might be described as a synthesis of what is already in the reader's head and what he or she learns from the text. Making inferences has been described as reading between the lines. Effective readers must be able to read beyond the text, to make interpretations beyond literal levels. Making inferences does not come naturally to many students; they must be taught how to integrate what they read with what they already know to interpret the text completely. A technique that some teachers like to use to teach inference is to bring in an unusual household item and invite students to guess what its purpose is.

Based on the research of Taffy Raphael (1986), three-level questioning is a strategy that helps us use effective questioning to guide students' thinking to higher levels, and that builds metacognition as well. What sets three-level questioning apart from traditional questioning is that it not only asks students to respond to different levels of questions, but teaches them that they get information in different ways when they read. Ultimately, we want students to question themselves as they read.

This technique involves asking students three types of questions about their reading:

1. **Right There** questions are literal questions that reflect information found directly in the text.
2. **On Your Own** questions ask the reader to evaluate or give his or her own opinion.
3. **Author and You** questions are inferential questions that require the reader to synthesize the information in the text with what she or he already knows in order to form new ideas.

Asking different levels of questions is intended to take students' thinking to higher levels. The three-level question technique extends thinking even further by having students think about *how* they got the information they needed to answer the questions.

Three-level questioning may be called 3-H questioning.

1. **Hand** questions are those you can put your hand right on the answer in the story.
2. **Heart** questions require you to answer from your heart. They ask for your opinion, how you feel, or what you would do.
3. **Head** questions ask you to combine what you read in the text with what you already know to come up with new thoughts. You can't put your hand right on the answer in the story, but you need to use the information in the text to come up with the answer.

Tip

Teach three-level questioning to promote inferential thinking. Visual reminders of three-level thinking are Hand questions, Heart questions, and Head questions.

Predicting and Confirming

Predicting involves making educated guesses about what will come next in the story. It is, in a way, a form of inferring, as readers must apply what they read in the text to what they already know in order to formulate their predictions. Demonstrate to students that predicting helps us attend to the information in the text and gives a focus for our reading.

If we want predicting to be an effective reading strategy, we need to revisit our predictions frequently throughout the reading. As we read, we have to think about whether the new information confirms our predictions or leads us to change them. It is important to convince students that there is nothing wrong with making an incorrect prediction, as long as it is supported by the text. Stories often deliberately take unexpected turns; that's what makes the story interesting! The important thing is to use the text to make informed predictions and to make adjustments in our predictions as we gain new information from our reading.

In a Guided Reading lesson, direct the students to stop at two or three strategic places in the text to confirm or adjust their predictions. The Predict and Confirm Organizer on page 120 may be used to help students make decisions about their predictions and find evidence from the text to support these decisions.

Visualizing

For many readers, reading a book is like watching a movie in their minds. For others, the concept of connecting words on a page to pictures in their minds must be explicitly taught. When students visualize what they read, they are making meaning of text by combining the words on the page with what they already know to create a picture in their minds. In fact, visualizing is a form of making inferences with mental pictures instead of words.

In picture books and beginning-reading texts, the illustrations contain essential support for the text. We need to teach students to "read" the information in pictures and talk about how different types of graphics help us understand both fiction and non-fiction text.

Stop and Sketch

As readers become more sophisticated, their texts contain fewer illustrations. Stop and Sketch is a good activity for Guided Reading. Have students put their STOP signs at a strategic spot in the text. When they have read the designated section of text, they stop and quickly sketch the picture that the reading creates in their minds.

Graphic Organizers

Graphic organizers help students create a visual representation of information in a text. They are particularly effective with reluctant learners, who may be intimidated by writing on a blank page. Graphic organizers range from the simple Venn Diagram to complex webs and charts. Examples include:

- A Venn Diagram (see BLM page 113) is used to compare two different elements.
- Webs (see BLM page 121) may be used to chart relationships among words, characters, or concepts.
- A story graph invites readers to plot the excitement or suspense level of various events in the story (see BLM page 122).

Synthesizing

When we use the strategy of *synthesis,* we transform the content of our reading into another form. Transforming helps us understand and remember what we read. We need to combine what is already in our background knowledge, or our schema, with what we learn from the reading to create a new form. Some ways to synthesize what we read might include

1. **Writing**—reports, poems, letters, journal entries, opinion pieces
2. **Performance**—presenting the material as a readers theatre, role drama, or improvisation
3. **Discussion**—sharing ideas with others
4. **Mind Map**—combining visual images with words
5. **Multimedia**—using computer technology to synthesize information in many ways

Fix-it Chart

If comprehension fails…

…ignore that section of text and read on

…look ahead

…make a prediction and read on

…go back and reread some of the text

Predict and Confirm Organizer

Before reading… What do you think will happen in this section of the text?	Why do you think so?
Read to page _______ What do you think is going to happen now?	Why do you think so?
Read to page _______ What do you think is going to happen now?	Why do you think so?

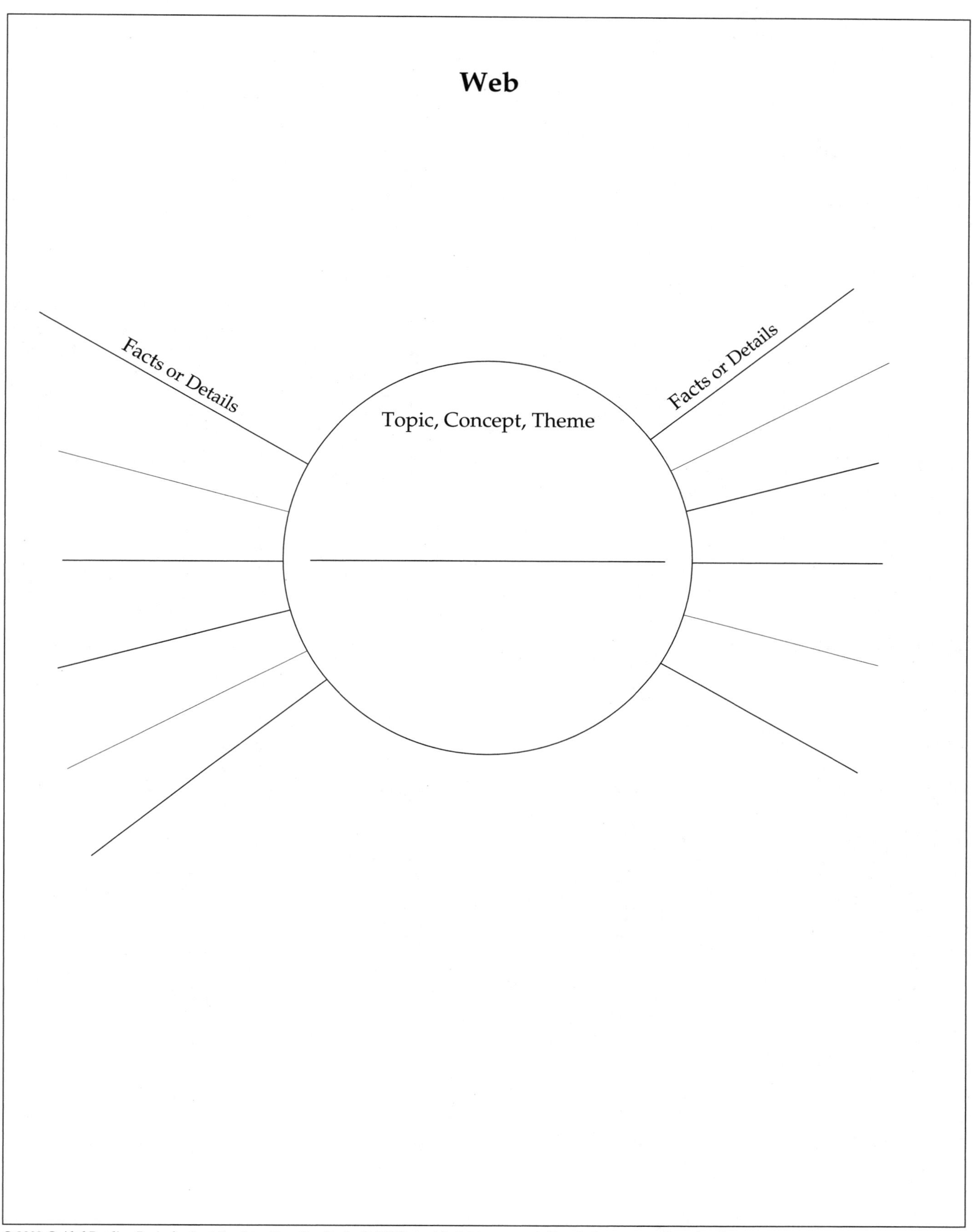
Web
Facts or Details
Facts or Details
Topic, Concept, Theme

Story Graph

Level of Excitement										
10										
9										
8										
7										
6										
5										
4										
3										
2										
1										
0										
Events from the Story										

Title ____

Author ____

13 Retelling and Responding to Texts

When we read, each of us brings a unique set of background experiences to the task. Reader Response Theory (Rosenblatt, 1978) tells us reading is a transaction between the reader and the text; that each reader interprets a text uniquely, depending on his or her knowledge, experience, perspectives, and understandings. When we invite readers to respond to reading, we invite them to create and share their own understandings of the text.

The most basic level of reader response is the literal retelling, which asks students to recall as many details from the story as they can. This is an important strategy at the early reading level, as it builds foundations of comprehension and story structure that can be extended into inferential interpretations at higher levels.

Summarizing is a more sophisticated level of retelling, in that it involves analyzing the information in the story to extract only the key ideas. In order to summarize, the reader needs a comprehensive understanding of the story. The reader must be able to discern key ideas, combine ideas, and eliminate extraneous details.

The highest level of response is the synthesis of information from the text with the reader's own ideas. Whether it is a critique, an analysis, an interpretation, or a connection, the personal response is generally associated with higher-level thinking. Even the youngest readers can offer support for an opinion or make personal connections. We want to encourage our more sophisticated readers to extend their thinking with inferences and interpretations of the text.

Retelling

Retelling requires the reader to organize text information in order to provide a personal rendition of it. Retelling has been found to significantly improve story comprehension, sense of story structure, and oral language complexity (Koskinen et al, 1988, p. 892).

As a comprehension strategy, retelling

- encourages readers to attend to the meaning of the text.
- reinforces elements of story structure, such as characters, setting, and plot
- requires readers to distinguish between key ideas and supporting details
- encourages communication and oral language development

As an assessment strategy, retelling

- demonstrates what the student understands and remembers about the story
- reveals what the student considers important about the story
- indicates what students know about story structure and literary language
- demonstrates the students' vocabulary and oral language development

Retellings may be oral or written, but oral retellings allow the child to focus on the story rather than the writing. Emergent and early readers should be expected to retell stories orally; written retellings may be used with more advanced readers. Observing an oral retelling enables the teacher to observe the student's behavior during retelling and to provide any necessary prompting.

Take time to teach! It is important to teach students how to retell a story, and what will be expected of their retelling.

It is important to teach students how to retell a story, and what will be expected of their retelling. Group retellings of read-alouds and shared book experiences can build comprehension strategies and understanding of story elements. Graphic organizers or props such as pictures or puppets may also be used to aid retelling.

Tools for Retelling

SHAPE-GO MAP

The Shape-Go Map below was created by Vicki Benson and Carrice Cummings (2000) to help readers organize their thinking for retelling. The triangle, a square, and a circle, represent the beginning, middle, and end of a story. For young students, the shapes can be color coded using traffic-light colors: green for Beginning, yellow for Middle, and red for End.

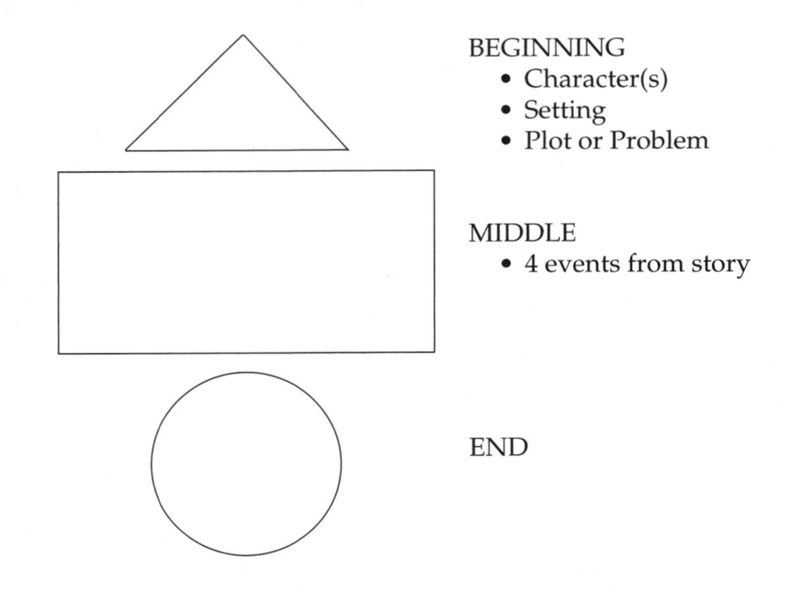

From *The Power of Retelling* by Vicki Benson and Carisse Cummings (Wright Group, 2000).

The three sides of the triangle are a reminder to identify the characters, setting, and plot or problem. The four sides of the rectangle remind the reader to tell about four key events in the story. The circle at the end reminds the reader that the end of the story should circle back to the beginning and solve the problem.

STORY MAP

A Story Glove is a retelling aid that can be made simply and inexpensively by drawing symbols of different literary elements (character, problem, solution) on the fingers of a gardening glove.

A story map can be any form of graphic organizer that guides the student in identifying the elements of the story.

- Story Stars (see BLM page 127) remind students of rising action in a story.
- Using the Story House on page 128, students are able to sketch each story element in the windows of the house. Fold back the flaps of the windows and

glue another piece of paper behind the house, so you can open the windows to see the ideas beneath.

GROUP RETELLING GAME

Creative dramatics may be used to act out a story as another form of retelling. Use puppets and other props to enhance the retelling.

Create a game card set with prompts such as those in the table on page 129. Each member of the group draws one or more cards until all the cards are distributed. Students take turns retelling their assigned parts of the story.

STORY SOUVENIRS

You can extend school reading experiences by sending home story souvenirs, simple mementos of a book read in class, to remind the children to retell the story to their parents. Some examples of story souvenirs might be a feather to represent a story about a bird, or a candle for a story about a birthday party. A response form is sent home to inform the parents of the procedure, and for parents to record the children's comments about the book. The students get to keep the souvenir as a memento of the book.

Using Retelling to Assess Comprehension

Retelling should be used as an assessment tool only after students have been taught how to retell a story and what is expected of them. One way to assess a retelling is to use a checklist such as the one found on page 130. Another is to have a copy of the text on hand and highlight elements of the story as the student retells it.

Before the reading, let the student know that you will ask her or him to tell you about the story when finished reading.

Some tips for using retelling as a comprehension/assessment tool:

- *Teach students how to retell and what the expectations are before reading.*
- *Scaffold students with prompts or questions if necessary.*
- *Allow students to revisit the text as they retell.*
- *Ensure that the texts are not beyond the students' reading level, unless the retelling is from a read-aloud.*
- *Use props, such as puppets or pictures, to aid retelling.*

After the student has read the story, you might say, "Pretend that I've never heard this story and tell me everything about it," or "Pretend you are telling this story to a friend who has never heard it."

If the retelling is incomplete, you may want to assist the reader to recall additional details. For example, if he or she is having trouble getting started, you might prompt with, "This story is about..."

If a student stops before giving all key information, encourage him or her to continue with prompts such as

- "What comes next?"
- "Then what?"
- "Tell me more about..."
- "What else do you remember?"

There is no reason not to allow students to revisit the text or use pictures to assist their retelling. Remember that the purpose of the retelling is to judge whether students understand the text, not just what they remember from the first reading. If readers have been focusing on decoding during the first reading, they may need to reread certain parts to refresh their memories.

Summarizing

Summarizing takes retelling a step further, in that it asks the reader to organize, synthesize, and analyze ideas for degree of importance. A summary does not include every detail from the story; instead it provides an overview of key ideas.

One way to teach summarizing is to record students' ideas as they tell all the parts of the story they can remember. Then take a look at the ideas and talk about which ones can go together under a more general statement, and which ones may be unnecessary for an overview. For example, you have just read "The Three Little Pigs" and the students recount the following ideas from the story.

> There were three pigs who were brothers.
> They each wanted to build a house.
> The first pig built his house out of straw.
> A wolf came along and blew the house down.
> The second pig built his house out of sticks.
> The wolf blew it down too.
> The third pig built his house out of bricks.
> The wolf tried and tried but he couldn't blow the house down.
> He tried to come down the chimney.
> The pigs built a fire in the chimney and the wolf landed in a pot of hot water.
> The pigs lived happily ever after.

Talk to the students about which ideas might be combined together and which ones aren't really necessary to a summary of the story. You may even want to use a scaffold like this: "This story is about ... who.... " Remind them that you don't need every detail in a summary, but you must give the key ideas.

> This story is about three pigs who wanted to build houses for themselves. The first two pigs built houses out of straw and sticks, and the wolf blew them down. The third pig's house was made of bricks and the wolf couldn't blow it down. When the wolf tried to come down the chimney, he landed in a pot of hot water, and that was the end of the wolf.

The summary provides a comprehensive overview of the text, by addressing only the salient points of the story and synthesizing supporting details into more general statements.

Personal Response

When inviting written responses to reading, you need to model and guide your students in the same way that you teach other concepts. If you want more than a literal retelling, demonstrate for your students what you're looking for. One way is to think aloud as you model a response. Then you can guide students in the collaborative writing of responses to a shared reading experience. This model helps students know how to respond effectively to a text. The rubric on page 132 is a guideline for teaching and evaluating literary responses.

Comparing Responses

Another effective strategy for teaching literature response is to share three or four samples of responses of differing qualities, and then work with students to identify what makes one better than another.

> 1. *The Paper Bag Princess* is a story about a princess who was being attacked by a dragon. The prince was supposed to save her, but instead she saved him. And then she wouldn't marry him.

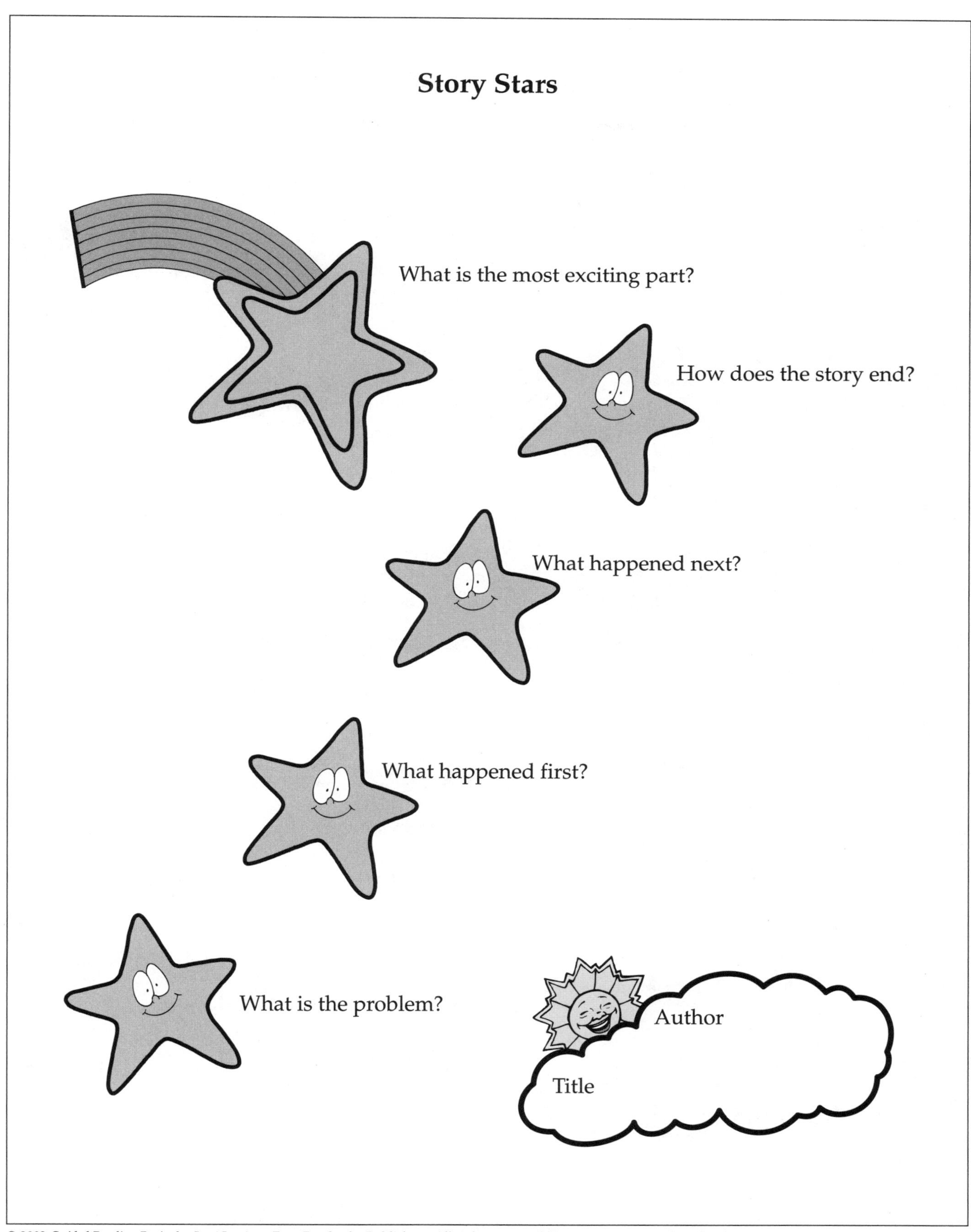
Story Stars
What is the most exciting part?
How does the story end?
What happened next?
What happened first?
What is the problem?
Author
Title

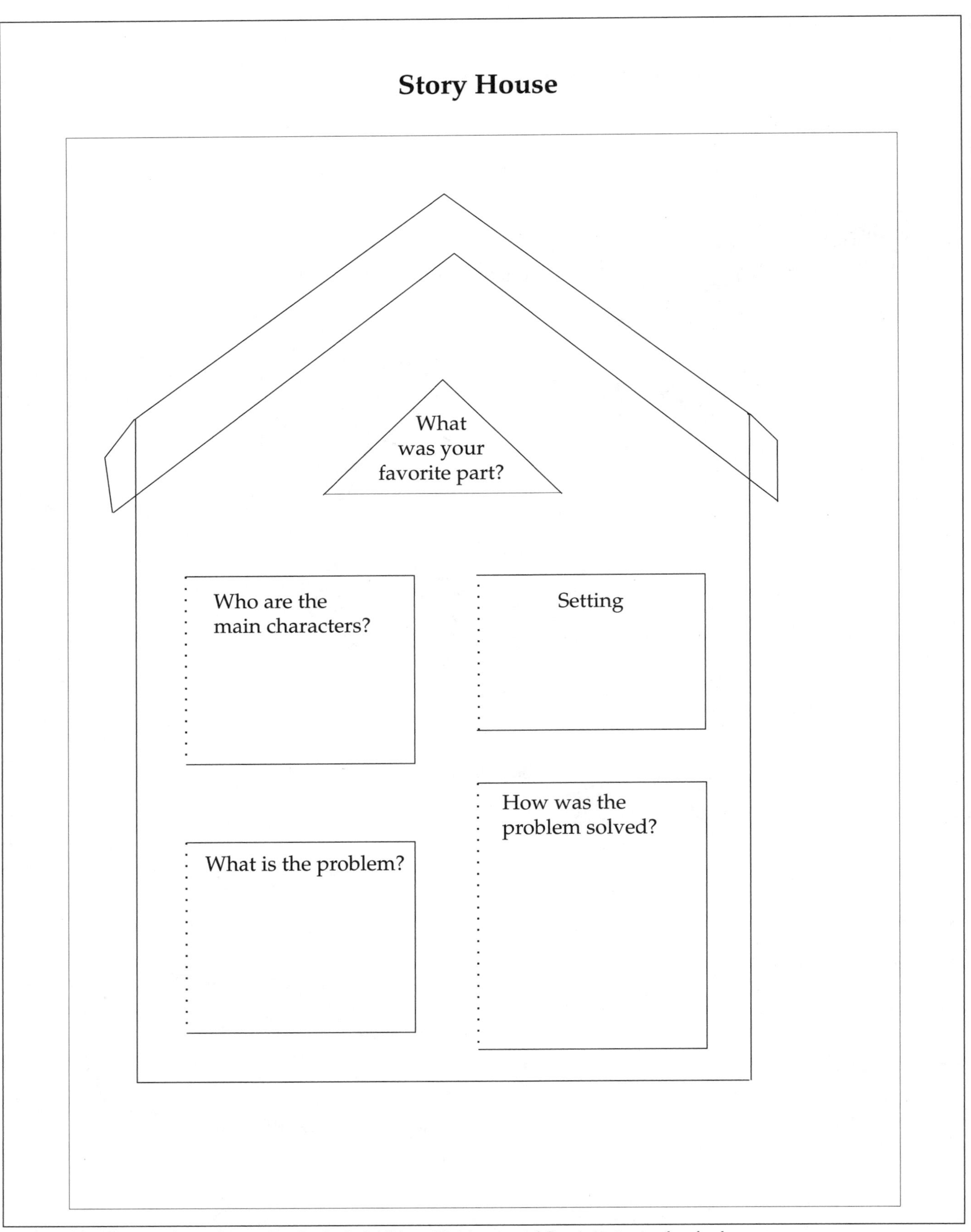
Story House
What was your favorite part?
Who are the main characters?
Setting
How was the problem solved?
What is the problem?

Group Retelling Game

1. This story is about…	2. The main character is…
3. His/her problem is…	4. The first thing that happens is…
5. The second thing that happens is…	6. The problem is solved when…
7. At the end of the story…	8. I liked the part where….

Checklist for Evaluating Retelling

Student's Name: ______________________ *Date:* ______________________

____

Title of Passage: ____

____

Unaided Retelling

❏ Gives general ideas, has gist of the story

❏ Includes all key events

❏ Tells events in proper sequence

❏ Includes important details

❏ Uses words and phrases from the text

❏ Rephrases and uses own words

❏ Makes inferences

❏ Makes connections and personal observations

Aided Retelling

❏ Used general prompts

Used specific questions about

❏ Setting

❏ Characters

❏ Main events

❏ Beginning (Problem)

❏ Conclusion (Solution)

❏ Details/Specific Information

2. *The Paper Bag Princess* is a story about a princess who saved a prince from the dragon instead of the other way around. I thought it was funny because she called Prince Harold a lazy bum.

3. *The Paper Bag Princess* is like a fairy tale because it has a princess and a prince and a dragon. It reminds me of *Prince Cinders* because in that book the characters were also the opposite of what you would expect. I like reading these kinds of books because they are funny and surprise you. You don't know what's going to happen till the end.

4. *The Paper Bag Princess* is a story about how a princess saves a prince from a dragon, then she doesn't want to marry him in the end. What makes it funny is the way the author describes the characters, just the opposite to what you would find in regular fairy tales. The princess is brave and cool but the prince is a loser. The author does a good job of making sure we don't know what's going to happen till the end. I enjoyed reading this book because I couldn't predict what was going to happen.

Have the students read each response and decide which was the most effective and why. Talk about how they can use these models for writing their own responses.

Graphic Organizers for Personal Responses

Here are some ideas for different forms of reading response. The advantage of using graphic organizers is that they provide a scaffold to guide students in their writing.

Be sure to model each of these organizers using a shared, modeled, or interactive writing strategy before expecting students to complete them independently. Ultimately, of course, we want to wean students from reliance on these scaffolds and construct their own responses.

SOS: SUMMARY, OPINION, SUPPORT

See the graphic organizer on page 133. In the first box, students retell the key points of the story. In the second box, they give an opinion elicited from the text. Did you like the story or not? Did you agree or disagree with the main idea? In the last box, students provide support for the opinion.

OWL: OBSERVE, WONDER, LINK TO LIFE

The OWL strategy (see page 134) invites students to tell what they notice or learned from the story, what they wonder about, and what personal connections they make.

TWO-COLUMN NOTES

This simple response format (see page 135) requires readers to respond to specific ideas or quotes from the story. They choose words, sentences, or ideas from the story to write in the left-hand column. Then in the right-hand column, they write their thoughts, questions, and connections relating to those ideas.

THE THREE R'S: RETELL, RELATE, RESPOND

In the Three R's Response (see page 136), students start by giving an overview of the story. Then they tell what they relate or connect to. Finally they give a personal response—how they felt, what they agreed with, what their opinion of the text was.

Rubric for Literature Response

	Exemplary	*Very Good*	*Good*	*Needs Help*
Reaction to Text	Provides in-depth exploration of own reactions, with thoughtful support from text	Gives simple descriptions of own reactions, with support from text	Describes parts that were "liked" or "disliked" with some support	A simple retelling of story, or description of what was "liked" or "disliked" without support
Making Personal Responses	Makes thoughtful, insightful connections to self, to other texts, and to bigger issues	Makes strong connections to personal experience and to other texts	Makes obvious or mundane personal connections to key ideas	Makes no personal connections, or makes connections unrelated to text
Interpretation of Text	Sophisticated inferences are described and supported with examples from text	Evidence of understanding and reflection on key ideas within the text	Summarizes key ideas in the text	Has trouble identifying key ideas in the text
Insight into Author's Craft: • theme • language • characters • mood	Compares different authors' styles; notes literary devices such as suspense, point of view	Recognizes and explains elements of craft, such as how the author creates mood	Can recognize some elements of craft, such as character development and interesting language	Is unable to identify elements of style or craft

SOS Response

Summary
Opinion
Support for Opinion

OWL Response

Observe

What do you notice or remember about the text?

onder

What do you wonder about?

Link to Life

What does the text remind you of?

Two-Column Notes

Words or ideas from the text	*Your own thoughts, questions or connections to those ideas*

Three R's Response

Retell the story in your own words.

Relate to your own life.

React with your opinions.

14 Using Non-Fiction

Elementary-school reading programs have traditionally been dominated by narrative texts. That's why most of our children learn to cope quite effectively with literary reading. But when they reach upper grades and encounter textbooks and research materials, even competent readers may flounder.

As teachers, from the earliest levels we have a responsibility to expose our students to a balance of forms and genres of texts: not just traditional tales, realistic fiction, fantasy, and science fiction, but also informational texts, and procedural and persuasive writing. As Linda Hoyt says, "In an information age where the volume of world knowledge is expanding at such a dramatic rate, we can no longer support the old adage of 'learning to read' then 'reading to learn'." (2000, p. 195)

The Guided Reading Lesson with informational text has the same form as that for narrative text.

Before Reading: book introduction to establish context and introduce key vocabulary

During Reading: Scaffolding students as they read

After Reading: Revisiting the text to reinforce strategy use and extend learning

This means we have to teach the special strategies required in reading for information. Reading informational text presents all the challenges of narrative text, as well as several other challenges unique to the genre:

- technical vocabulary specific to the topic
- dense concentration of facts and details
- assumption that the reader has some background knowledge of the topic
- unique writing conventions and styles

However, most informational text for young readers also provides a number of conventions that provide supports not present in narrative text, such as

- headings and subheadings
- visuals: pictures, graphics, charts, bullets
- special fonts and styles: italics, boldface
- topic sentences
- introductions and summaries
- organizational matter: table of contents, index, glossary
- support for complex vocabulary: definitions, examples, comparisons
- information provided in small chunks

Until recently, most non-fiction material was beyond the scope of beginning readers. However, a surge of publishing for early reading has included more and more wonderful "info-texts" for even the youngest readers. There is no reason why informational texts cannot be part of the Guided Reading program right from the earliest levels.

The Guided Reading Lesson Using Non-fiction

Whether the texts are narrative or informational, the Guided Reading lesson will be structured in the same way. Start with a book introduction to set a context, make connections and predictions, and introduce vocabulary. Guide and scaffold the readers as they negotiate the text. After the reading, provide opportunities for revisiting the text, as well as for discussion and extensions that build reading, writing, and thinking skills.

Before Reading: Book Introduction

Two things are particularly important for preparing to read informational text: accessing prior knowledge and introducing unfamiliar vocabulary. Informational text often assumes certain knowledge of concepts and vocabulary on the part of the reader. Students must be explicitly taught to mine the recesses of their minds for that background information, so they can connect the new learning to what they already know. Whether the topic is mummies or moon exploration, your students will already know something about it. Begin with that. It will guide you in making decisions about what they need to learn next.

Introducing vocabulary is also important in preparing students for informational reading. A misunderstanding of even one or two key words can affect the comprehension of the entire passage. Pre-teaching key vocabulary makes a difficult text accessible to more readers. For example, the passage "A World of Chocolate," found on page 150, is measured at a Grade 5.2 reading level, based on conventional readability formulas such as Flesch-Kincaid. But simply teaching the words "chocolate" and "cocoa" makes the text accessible to students in Grade 2 or 3.

Tip

Have students sketch a "map" of the page, noting where headings, graphics, text boxes, etc. are found.

The book introduction should also draw students' attention to the unique structures, or conventions, of informational text. Often a single page of informational text for readers may contain a variety of headings, graphics, and text boxes. Negotiating this material can be overwhelming for the young reader. During the picture walk or book preview, point out features such as headings, captions, visuals, and the table of contents. This structural knowledge is increasingly important as texts become more sophisticated.

Setting a purpose for reading has particular importance with informational texts. Reading for information often entails adjusting the speed of reading and even the style of reading. Sometimes we skim over the material quickly for a general impression. Sometimes we have to carefully read word by word and line by line to recall every detail. And sometimes we can even skip the parts that do not pertain to our purpose for reading. Understanding *why* we are reading a particular text helps us decide *how* to read it.

During Reading: Scaffolded Reading

The book introduction should have provided enough scaffolds for the readers to access the text without difficulty. However, you may want to emphasize certain during-reading strategies to encourage students to monitor their own comprehension and to assimilate new information from the text:

- skimming and scanning for information
- using vocabulary cues to meaning
- distinguishing key information from supporting detail
- using conventions of informational text to support comprehension
- predicting and confirming
- self-questioning

After Reading

Sometimes the reading of the text will be an end in itself. The processes of predicting, anticipating, and negotiating the text are valuable learning experiences for the young reader. At other times, you will want to work with the information from the reading or extend the learning with further research. Teach students to take notes, to compile facts, and to synthesize information into research projects. This brings the skills and strategies of reading for information to real life.

Non-fiction at Different Reading Levels

Non-fiction for Emergent Readers

Informational texts for emergent-level readers look very much like narrative texts for emergent readers. Often they contain photographs and illustrations, with simple labels and sentence patterns.

Areas of focus for teaching will be the same as for narrative texts:

- concepts about print
- high-frequency words
- letter–sound concepts

Mother Owl and her baby are up in the tree.

Mother Beaver and her baby are down in the pond.

Mothers and Babies by Jennifer Low, illustrated by Effie Balmoenos; Curriculum Plus, 2001. Reprinted with permission.

In this sample from *Mothers and Babies,* for example, note the sentence pattern, and the repeated use of the words "up" and "down." In addition to an extensive picture walk to reinforce the pattern and introduce vocabulary, you may want to use sentence cards: students can match the anchor words to those in the text, and reassemble cut-up sentences to match those in the text.

Non-fiction for Early Readers

At the early reading level, we can start to teach our students the differences between narrative and informational texts: narrative texts tell a story, while informational texts provide facts about a topic. We can teach students that in stories, they predict what is going to happen next, while in informational texts, they predict what they might learn next. Take time to compare a story and an info text. For example, in introducing an informational text about raccoons, you might show the students a familiar fiction text about raccoons, such as *The Kissing Hand,* to compare the text structure and content.

Tip

Keep a classroom chart of non-fiction conventions, refer to it frequently, and add to it as new conventions are discovered. (See page 150 for more details.)

BEFORE READING

Early texts begin to exhibit some of the conventions of informational writing: subheadings, visuals with captions, glossary, and table of contents. Encourage students to identify text structures that help them understand and remember what they read. When you preview a text, be sure to draw students' attention to conventions like headings and illustrations, and use them to make predictions about what they will learn in the text.

Because info-texts for early readers may contain complex vocabulary and concepts, you will want to use the book introduction to access prior knowledge, pre-teach vocabulary, and establish a context for reading. In early-level texts, new vocabulary is generally repeated several times; prepare students for this vocabulary in the book introduction and preview. The K-W-L-S chart described on page 145 is a wonderful collaborative activity for activating prior knowledge and setting purposes for reading.

DURING READING

As students read, listen and take note of strategy use. If students make miscues, use the same prompts as with narrative text: Does it make sense? Does it sound right? Does it match the print? Regardless of the text genre, this is the stage at which students are learning to use cueing strategies flexibly and to monitor their own reading.

You may want to guide the students to read chunks of text at a time. For example, you may ask them to "read to the part that describes what a raccoon looks like" or "read to the part that tells about different places that a raccoon will make its home." This helps them monitor their own comprehension, and think about the meaning as they read.

AFTER READING

Ask the students to recall reading strategies they used during reading. Offer your own observations about strategy use that you noticed. Ask students questions like, "How did the pictures help you read?"

Because of the density of information in an info text, you will want to revisit the text to discuss and record facts. Encourage students to go back into the texts to review and recall the information. Provide other texts on the same topic for those students who want to do further research.

Non-fiction for Developing Readers

Developing readers have many reading strategies in place. They use cueing strategies flexibly. They can understand and retell what they read. Now they need to extend their independence, build their repertoire of strategies, and learn to read "between and beyond" the lines.

Because complex vocabulary is not repeated and reinforced in texts for developing readers, it is important that students get advance exposure to all the words they will need to know in the text. As we discussed in Chapter 11, simply defining new words will not help students assimilate them into their existing knowledge banks. A Concept Map or a Word Sort (see Chapter 11) helps students connect technical vocabulary to existing knowledge and integrate new vocabulary in a meaningful way.

More text structures are evident in developing texts and it is important to continue to discuss how these conventions help the reader. Taking time to guide students through structures like a table of contents, glossary, or index provides them with increasing strategies for independent reading of informational text.

Give students opportunities for guided practice in skimming and scanning to ensure they understand when to use each of these reading styles.

Using different styles and rates of reading is important at this stage. Demonstrate for students how to skim for overall impressions and how to scan for specific details.

After reading, provide opportunities to revisit the text to recall facts and use them in meaningful ways. There are many forms of informational reports that developing readers may prepare as a means of synthesizing non-fiction reading.

Non-fiction for Fluent Readers

We hope that fluent readers will independently apply the before-, during-, and after-reading strategies that we guided them through in previous stages. We also want them to extend their strategies in order to be able to access and use texts of increasing difficulty. Reading the text will no longer be an end in itself; the fluent reader reads informational text to understand the world and to use the information for specific purposes. Therefore, we want to encourage strategies that extend thinking and that enable the reader to read critically and responsively. Usually we want our fluent readers to make some sort of writing extension from their reading experience.

Teaching Strategies for Informational Text

Before-reading Strategies

ANTICIPATION GUIDE

An Anticipation Guide is intended to get students thinking about the information they will encounter in the text. Often an anticipation guide will consist of a series of true/false or agree/disagree statements that the reader must respond to before reading the text. After reading, the reader revisits the statements to think about whether his or her responses have changed as a result of the reading.

Of course, it is not important for the reader to have the "right" responses before reading. The statements are intended to create a context for the reading and to guide the reader's thinking as he or she reads. Revisiting the statements after reading enables readers to synthesize what they have learned. Making some of the statements ambiguous or partially correct generates good discussion among the students and forces them to think about their thinking.

WORD SORT

The Word Sort, also described in Chapter 11, involves selecting a collection of words from the passage the students are about to read. The students work in groups to decide which words go together and why, organizing the words into categories. There is no limit to the number of words in a category, nor is there a single correct way to sort the words. A variation of the Word Sort is to have students create sentences from pairs of words in the group.

Group discussion helps clarify the meaning of the words for all the students, and establishes a context for reading. Again, it is the conversations around the process that are important, rather than the way the words are sorted. After sorting the words, the students are asked to predict what the passage will be about, based on the words they have sorted.

Non-fiction Guided Reading Lessons at Each Level of Development

Level	*Suggestions for Lesson Focus*
Emergent	Concepts about print; concept of "word" High-frequency words Using letter–sound correspondences
Early	Structures and conventions of informational text Comparing fiction and non-fiction Using vocabulary supports Accessing prior knowledge Setting a purpose for reading Flexible use of cueing strategies Recalling facts
Developmental	Reading in different styles for different purposes Self-monitoring comprehension Distinguishing main ideas and supporting details Predicting from topic sentences Looking for vocabulary cues Beginning to use text structures
Fluent	Anticipating and predicting Using text structures Appreciating different opinions Recognizing bias Synthesizing information

A Word Sort for the "A World of Chocolate" passage, on page 150, might look like this:

chocolate	cocoa	sugar	liquid
bitter	sweet	flavor	milk
powdered	candy bars	roasted	crushed

TEXT PREVIEW

Whether students are reading an entire text or an excerpt, they should be taught to pay attention to the supports and challenges they are likely to encounter. Sometimes, the many visual and graphic supports in today's info texts can be distracting to an unsophisticated reader. But even beginning readers can learn how to make use of these valuable tools. In previewing a section of text, the reader should attend to the following four key elements of the text in order to make predictions about the reading:

1. **Overall Layout** Take a minute to examine how the page is organized: what kinds of visuals there are and where they are located, what the headings say, and whether there are any unique text structures such as bold or italic faces. Talk about how these supports help the reader understand what he or she is reading. You may even want to sketch the layout of the page: Where are the pictures, headings, captions, text boxes, etc.?
2. **Headings** Unlike narrative text, informational text contains headings that break the text into chunks and give clues about the content. Different type sizes and faces identify headings at different levels.
3. **Visuals** Info texts for young readers contain many visual elements that add interest and information: photographs, illustrations, charts, maps, boxes, color, font variations. A quick survey of these elements can give valuable clues to the content of the text. Sidebars and pull-outs are visual elements that provide textual information.
4. **Introduction and Conclusion** The opening and closing paragraphs of a chapter or other section of informational text generally identify key ideas in that text.

K-W-L-S

K-W-L-S (see BLM on page 145) is a strategy that helps students access prior knowledge and set a purpose for reading. Based on the K-W-L strategy developed by Donna Ogle (1986), this activity includes before-reading and after-reading components.

Tip

Instead of writing the students' ideas on the chart, write them on sticky notes so they may be moved around, as necessary. After reading, all of the facts may be combined and sorted into categories.

Before reading, students discuss and record what they already Know about the topic in the *K* column, and what they Want to find out in the *W* column. The Want column will comprise questions about the topic that might be answered from the reading. Developing these questions also serves to set a purpose for reading.

After reading, record what was Learned in the *L* column. Often the reading will not provide answers to all of the questions, and it might even elicit more questions. These additional questions for further research should be recorded in the *S* column, as things the reader Still wants to know.

At first, complete the K-W-L-S chart together as a shared reading/writing activity. Gradually students can develop the independence to consider their own background knowledge and set purposes when they read.

During-reading Strategies

SKIM, SCAN, OR SKIP

Students need to learn that good readers read in different ways and at different rates, depending on the purpose for reading and the type of text. Both skimming and scanning involve running your eyes quickly over a page, attending to key words to get information, but they serve different purposes. Skimming entails gathering a general impression about a text, while scanning involves searching for specific information. In both of these processes, readers will skip sections of text that do not contain relevant information.

For many readers, it will be necessary to model and practise each of these styles of reading. Tell students the purpose of the strategy: "When I want to quickly get a general sense of what a section of text is about, I run my eyes quickly over the page without focusing on specific words. This is called 'skimming'." Ask students to pretend your finger is your eye as you run it down a page of text on a chart or overhead, not extending to the ends of lines, pausing at occasional key words but generally sweeping quickly over the text. Summarize what you have read in one or two sentences. Then have students practise the strategy in pairs. Work for speed and accuracy by having students time each other and summarize the text to their partners.

Repeat the activity with key words, having students scan for a specific piece of information. Finally, talk about when they might skip certain parts of information for specific purposes.

Repeat this lesson as frequently as needed by your Guided Reading groups to ensure that they develop these reading strategies. Be sure to use the terminology and encourage students to do so.

Tip

You can create hundreds of sticky notes from a single pad. Just use an X-acto knife to slice the pad into two or three strips.

CODING

Coding is one way of monitoring our own comprehension as we read. When students read informational texts, they are likely to encounter many facts they already know, some facts they didn't know before, and the occasional fact that is particularly interesting or unique. Provide students with small sticky notes (from their Reading Tool Kits, as described in Chapter 5) for marking significant passages. For example, a student could use a sticky note with a check mark (✓) Facts I Already Knew, a star (*) for Facts I Learned, and an exclamation mark (!) for Amazing Facts. You may want to limit the number of sticky notes each student receives, or invite them to note just one example of each type of fact. Different texts will lend themselves to different codes. Work with your students to create the codes that suit each reading best.

Tip

Create a classroom chart of signal words and keep adding to it as students discover new signals in their reading.

Vocabulary Signals

Non-fiction texts usually contain difficult or unusual vocabulary pertinent to the topic. But these texts also include supports for understanding those words, often providing clues right in the text. Sometimes a definition will be provided. Sometimes there are examples, comparisons, or restatements in the text. We can teach students to look for clues that these supports are in place.

Some of the ways informational text gives important information are

- by describing cause and effect
- by comparing or contrasting
- by providing answers or solutions
- by giving examples
- by providing an order or sequence

K-W-L-S Chart

Before Reading	
What I already **K**now	What I **W**ant to find out
After Reading	
What I **L**earned	What I **S**till Want to know

Adapted from Ogle, 1986.

Signal Words Chart

Cause/Effect	*Comparisons*	*Solutions or Answers*	*Examples*
Because Therefore So For this reason	As opposed to Similarly But On the other hand	The reason One may conclude The solution	For example Such as Like

TOPIC SENTENCES

One of the common structures of informational text is the topic sentence. Usually the first sentence in each paragraph provides an overview of what the paragraph is about, but occasionally the topic sentence is found at the end of the paragraph, or even somewhere in the middle. Find a paragraph with a strong topic sentence in your Guided Reading text. Write the topic sentence on a chart and invite students to predict what information they are likely to encounter in the paragraph. Talk about how topic sentences help them understand what they read.

Encourage the students to look for topic sentences as they read. You may want to guide them through several paragraphs, using the topic sentence to elicit predictions, then reading on to add information to their predictions.

After-reading Strategies

WHAT'S IMPORTANT? WHAT'S INTERESTING?

What's Important? What's Interesting? is a strategy to help students learn to distinguish key information from supporting details (Harvey and Goudvis, 2001). After reading, make a two-column chart. Invite students to share facts that they learned from the reading and, as each idea is shared, talk about whether that idea adds to our knowledge about the topic or just provides some interesting detail.

CONVENTIONS CHART

Keep an ongoing record of the features, or conventions, of non-fiction text. As students discover supports in the reading, revisit the chart and record any additions. Record examples from the text, where appropriate, and take note of how the author used these techniques to help the reader. Here are some examples from the "World of Chocolate" text on page 150.

Convention	*Example*	*How it helped*
Subheadings	"From Cocoa Beans to Chocolate"	• gives a hint about what is coming up in the next section of text

Convention	*Example*	*How it helped*
Picture with Caption	"Switzerland is a country in Europe that is famous for its chocolate."	• breaks up the text so it's easier to read • gives some background information to support information in the text
Word Signals	"cocoa, which is…"	• defines a difficult word

Summarizing

Summarizing narrative text is discussed in Chapter 9 on Guided Reading for Fluent Readers. Summarizing informational text involves recounting the key ideas from a text concisely and succinctly. Summarizing encourages students to distil the main points of the text and to combine ideas into categories. Here are four steps to developing a summary:

1. Start with a topic sentence that gives an overview of the information in the text.
2. List all the key ideas you can recall from the text. Review them and cross out ideas that are supporting detail and do not add to the main idea.
3. See which ideas you can combine. Find a general or categorical statement you can make about the group of ideas.
4. Organize the ideas in a logical order.

SYNTHESIZING

Synthesizing involves taking all your ideas on a topic—from your previous knowledge, from your reading, from other experiences—and applying them to a new concept or structure. For example, writing a report involves synthesizing ideas from a variety of sources. There are many different reporting formats for students to use, ranging from a pattern like The Important Thing About… on page 151 to more formal essay frameworks.

Some options for short reports:

Tip

Focus the report topic as tightly as possible and to keep the report short, no more than a couple of pages. Remember that both process and product are paramount at this stage. Shorter texts lend themselves more easily to revision and editing strategies.

Reporting Vests for young students made out of large paper grocery bags: Glue pictures and captions, or draw, right on the vest. Then wear your vest as a guide when you present the report orally.

Telephone Poems: Write the digits of your telephone number in a column. Now write a seven-line free-verse poem about your topic, with your telephone number as the guide for how many words to write in that line. Use "0" as a bonus line, with as many words as you want.

Five False Facts: Get ten 3" x 5" cards. Find five true facts about your topic and write each one on a separate card, then illustrate the cards. On the other five cards, write five facts that are *not* true about your topic. Put your cards in a decorated envelope and exchange with a friend, to see if each of you can separate the true and false facts.

Investigation, which Linda Hoyt describes as a one-page overview that enables students to "dip their toes" in a topic: After reading about a topic of interest, create a report consisting of short chunks of text integrated with pictures, with a border around the page to create a strong visual as well as informational impact.

Brochure: Use a desktop publishing program to create a fold-over brochure about your topic. Make sure to look at plenty of samples to help plan what text to include, what kinds of graphics to use, and the overall layout of your brochure.

Sample Lesson Using Non-fiction

Here is a sample Guided Reading lesson for fluent readers, using a short article titled "A World of Chocolate," found on page 150. Caution! This reading may provoke a snack attack!

Before Reading

Introduce the reading, starting with the title. Find out what students notice about the word "chocolate," drawing attention to correct pronunciation with three syllables and silent *-e* at the end of the word. Ask what strategies they might use to remember the spelling. Point out two other words in this article that look very similar—"cocoa" and "cacao"—noting that readers have to pay close attention to the differences. After teaching how to pronounce these two words, leave it to the students to figure how their meanings are similar and different from the text.

ANTICIPATION GUIDE

An Anticipation Guide is a set of statements about the reading, which students must read and then decide whether they are true or not. This activity has the added value of introducing concepts and vocabulary that are necessary background for the students. Have students work individually or in pairs to respond to each statement before reading.

Before Reading		*After Reading*
__Agree __Disagree	People around the world have always loved chocolate.	__Agree __Disagree
__Agree __Disagree	Chocolate grows on trees.	__Agree __Disagree
__Agree __Disagree	Milk chocolate was created by mixing milk and chocolate.	__Agree __Disagree
__Agree __Disagree	Chocolate was discovered about 500 years ago.	__Agree __Disagree

During Reading

Move from the Anticipation Guide into the reading: "Now that you have thought about which of these statements you think are true, go on and read the whole article to see if you were right. At the end, we will talk about whether you changed your minds about any of the ideas."

As students read, circulate among them and ask them to read certain passages to assess their fluency and comprehension.

After Reading

Revisit the Anticipation Guide to see if anyone changed their True/False statements at the end of reading. Talk about the purpose of the exercise and the fact that whether they were right or wrong at the outset is not important.

This Anticipation Guide is designed to generate discussion. It could be argued that chocolate does or doesn't grow on trees: it is made from a bean that grows on a tree. Is the third statement true or false if you need butter and chocolate syrup as well as milk to create milk chocolate? The key is that students learn to support their arguments.

You may want to introduce a discussion of theme and bias by asking: "Do you think this writer likes chocolate? How do you think the article might sound different if it was written by someone who did not like chocolate?"

There are many delicious books about chocolate that students could read to extend this Guided Reading lesson. Treat the students to a tasting experience with different types of chocolate, such as cocoa powder, milk chocolate, and dark chocolate. A survey of people's tastes might be part of a report on "The World's Favorite Flavor – Or Is It?"

Have students synthesize their background knowledge and opinions about chocolate with the new information from their reading by writing a response such as "The Important Thing about Chocolate" (see sample page 151) based on the pattern from *The Important Book* by Margaret Wise Brown.

Reading informational texts crosses the bridge between learning to read and reading to learn. As Leah told her mother after reading a text on snakes: "I didn't use to know anything about snakes, but now I'm an expert."

A World of Chocolate

Imagine a world with no chocolate! That's right. Five hundred years ago, no one in the world had tasted chocolate.

From Cocoa Beans to Chocolate

Cocoa beans are picked from the cacao tree.

Before that, people only had cocoa, which is a powder made from beans that grow on a tree. But cocoa beans do not taste good by themselves. They are bitter and turn your mouth brown.

In the 1500s, people first found out how to turn cocoa into chocolate. They roasted and crushed the cocoa beans. Then they mixed the beans with sugar and water to make liquid chocolate.

The World's Favorite Flavor

In 1856, people in Switzerland tried to add butter and milk to liquid chocolate. This was the first milk chocolate. Now it's the world's favorite flavor.

Switzerland is a country in Europe that is famous for its chocolate.

Chocolate Today

Today, chocolate comes in many different forms. There is hot cocoa to drink. There is powdered chocolate for baking. There is milk chocolate for candy bars. All over the world, people enjoy chocolate treats every day. Aren't we lucky to live today?

By Alex Kropp
Reprinted with permission

The Important Thing About...

The Important Thing about ______________ *is*

____

It is ____

____

It ____

____

It ____

____

And it ____

____

But the most important thing about __________ is___________________________

____

Adapted from *The Important Book* by Margaret Wise Brown.

CONCLUSION

What Research Tells Us about Differentiating Instruction

There has never been a more exciting time—nor a more challenging time—to be a teacher. Today we know more about how children learn to read, and how best to teach them, than ever before. Current research and practice on exemplary reading instruction affirm the principles of effective practice inherent in the Guided Reading model.

Pioneers in literacy research—such as Marie Clay, founder of Reading Recovery, and Russian psychologist Lev Vygotsky—remind us that learning is a process of constructing meaning. Dr. Clay defines reading as "a meaning-making, problem-solving activity which increases in power and flexibility the more it is practised" (1991, p. 6). Vygotsky theorized that there is a zone of "proximal development" between what a learner can do independently at a given moment and what he has the potential to do with expert support. Vygotsky saw the teacher's role as providing scaffolding to take students to a higher level of development.

The Guided Reading model provides the scaffolding that enables young readers to construct meaning from print. Students are provided with a text they cannot read independently but can access with expert support. This support includes an effective book introduction, sensitive scaffolding during reading that offers instruction at the point of need, and extension activities that reinforce strategic learning and extend thinking. Through this process, students develop the independent reading skills and strategies that enable them to make meaning from increasingly sophisticated texts.

The National Reading Panel in the United States (2000) conducted a meta-analysis of a large body of empirical research in reading instruction, and found support for five key literacy practices: phonemic awareness instruction, systematic phonics instruction, guided oral reading, vocabulary instruction, and comprehension strategy instruction. An effective Guided Reading lesson incorporates these elements at appropriate levels of development within the context of meaningful reading. As Dorothy Strickland reminds us, instruction in discrete skills should always be linked to the process of reading connected text.

Probably the greatest challenge for teachers today is the increasing diversity of students in their classrooms. Different cultural backgrounds, different home environments, different attitudes toward literacy and learning, and different learning needs all challenge us as teachers. How can we teach in such a way as to honor the unique strengths and needs of every student, while ensuring that each one is constantly scaffolded to higher levels of proficiency? A Guided Reading program lends itself naturally and effectively to meeting this challenge.

Differentiated instruction is a philosophy of teaching that strives to maximize each student's growth by providing learning experiences that take each student from his or her current level of development to higher levels of proficiency. It takes into account not just a student's abilities, but also his or her interests, learning styles, and readiness to learn. Some of the essential elements (Tomlinson, 2000) of differentiated instruction include

- respect for the differences and similarities among students
- ongoing assessment to guide instruction
- engaging students in meaningful learning experiences at all times
- focus on developing independent, strategic learners
- collaboration between teacher and students
- flexible grouping
- using a variety of instructional strategies and tools based on the varying needs and learning styles of the students.

As pointed out in this book, the Guided Reading lesson is different for students at different levels. It honors learners at many levels by ensuring that texts and activities provide a balance of challenge and support, using sensitive instruction that meets students at their point of need and scaffolds them to higher levels of development. Oral reading records, comprehension assessments, and anecdotal records inform the teacher about each student's progress and guide him or her in planning instruction and restructuring groups. Groups are changed frequently as students' needs change, and the needs-based Guided Reading group is only one form of grouping that students experience in their balanced literacy program. Students are taught to make choices and monitor their own learning through literacy centres and other independent learning tasks while the teacher is involved with other groups of students. And, most importantly, students learn to solve problems, apply strategies, use metacognition, and gradually increase their independence as readers and learners.

It is important to reiterate that Guided Reading is only one component of a total balanced literacy program. Our students have many literacy needs, which must be met through a variety of means. Your language arts program will also include shared reading; independent reading; interactive read-alouds; modeled, shared, and interactive writing; and writing workshop. The International Reading Association (1999) reminds us that "there is no single method or combination of methods that can successfully teach all children to read. Therefore, teachers must have a strong knowledge of multiple methods for teaching reading and a strong knowledge of the children in their care so they can create the appropriate balance of methods needed for the children they teach."

Our challenge as teachers is to provide instruction that meets the needs of all of our students, always offering them reading and writing experiences that engage and inform. We want our students to become competent and confident readers, readers who experience not only the value, but the joy of literacy. Our goal is to help build the skill and will to be lifelong readers, so that throughout their lives they continue to exhibit the same delight experienced by a first grader named Timmy on his very first day of school. That day, a wise teacher handed out a wordless alphabet book and together they negotiated the pictures representing each letter of the alphabet. As they closed the book, Timmy threw his hands in the air and shouted triumphantly, "I can read!" As teachers, we must do what we can to ensure that Timmy, and others like him, never lose that sense of confidence and delight in the written word.

Resources

Allen, J., *Words, Words, Words: Teaching Vocabulary in Grades 4–12.* York, ME: Stenhouse Publishers, 1999.

Benson, Vicki, and Cummins, Carrice, *The Power of Retelling: Developmental Steps for Building Comprehension.* New York, NY: Wright Group-McGraw Hill, 2000.

Bergeron, Bette S., and Bradbury-Wolff, Melody, *Teaching Reading Strategies in the Primary Grades.* NY: Scholastic Professional Books, 2002.

Calkins, Lucy McCormick, *The Art of Teaching Reading.* New York: Longman, 2001.

Clay, M..M., "Introducing a New Storybook to Young Readers" in *The Reading Teacher,* 45, 1991, pp. 264–73.

Cunningham, P. M., and Cunningham, J. W., "Making Words: Enhancing the Invented Spelling-Decoding Connection" in *The Reading Teacher,* 46:2, October 1992.

Cunningham, P. M., *Phonics they use: Words for reading and writing,* second edition. New York: Addison Wesley, 1999.

Depree, Helen, and Iverson, Sandra, *Early Literacy in the Classroom.* Richmond Hill ON: Scholastic Canada, 1994.

Diller, Debbie, *Literacy Work Stations: Making Centers Work.* Portland, ME: Stenhouse Publishers, 2003.

First Steps Reading Resource Book. Western Australia: Education Department of Western Australia, 1994.

Fountas, I., and Pinnell, G.S., *Guided Reading: Good First Teaching for All students.* Portsmouth, NH: Heinemann, 1996.

— *Matching books to readers: Using leveled books in guided reading, K–3.* Portsmouth, NH: Heinemann, 1999.

— *Guiding Readers and Writers in Grades 3–6.* Portsmouth, NH: Heinemann, 2001.

Goodman, K., *Ken Goodman On Reading.* Richmond Hill, ON: Scholastic Canada, 1996; and Portsmouth, NH: Heinemann, 1996.

Harvey, Stephanie, and Goudvis, Anne, *Strategies that work.* York, ME: Stenhouse Publishers, 2001.

Hoyt, Linda, *Snapshots: Literacy Minilessons Up Close.* Portsmouth, NH: Heinemann, 2000.

— *Making it Real: Strategies for Success with Informational Texts.* Portsmouth, NH: Heinemann, 2002.

International Reading Association, *Excellent Reading Teachers: A Position Statement of the International Reading Association.* Newark, DE: International Reading Association, 2000.

— *Using Multiple Methods of Beginning Reading Instruction: A Position Statement of the International Reading Association.* Newark, DE: International Reading Association, 1999.

Jamison Rog, L., and Burton, W., "Matching Readers and Texts" in *The Reading Teacher,* December 2000–January 2001.

Jamison Rog, L., "Fluency: The Forgotten Reading Strategy" in *Query: The Journal of the Saskatchewan Reading Council,* Winter 2002.

Johns, J., *Basic Reading Inventory.* Dubuque, Iowa: Kendall/Hunt Publishers, 2001.

Keene, E., and Zimmerman, S., *Mosaic of Thought.* Portsmouth, NH: Heinemann, 1998.

Koskinen, P., Gambrell L., Kapinus, B., and Heathington, B., "Retelling: A Strategy for Enhancing Students' Reading Comprehension" in *The Reading Teacher,* May 1988.

Lynch, Judy, *Word Learning, Word Making, Word Sorting.* NY: Scholastic, 2002.

McLaughlin, M., *Guided Comprehension in the Primary Grades.* Newark, DE: International Reading Association, 2003

Miller, D., *Reading with Meaning.* York, ME: Stenhouse, 2001.

National Reading Panel, *Teaching Children to Read: An Evidence Based Assessment of the Scientific Research Literatures on Reading and its implications for reading instruction.* Washington, DC: U.S. Department of Health and Human Services, 2000.

Ogle, D., "K-W-L; A teaching model that develops active reading of expository text" in *The Reading Teacher,* 39, 1986, pp. 564–70.

Opitz, Michael F., *Flexible Grouping in Reading.* New York: Scholastic Professional Books, 1998.

Paulson, N., and Nos, N., *Using Guided Reading to Strengthen Students' Reading Skills at the Emergent Level.* Bellevue, WA: Bureau of Education and Research, 2001.

Raphael, Taffy, "Teaching children Question-Answer Relationships, revisited" in *The Reading Teacher,* 39, 1986, pp. 516–22.

Rosenblatt, L., *The Reader, the text and the poem: The transactional theory of the literary work.* Carbondale, IL: Southern Illinois University Press, 1978.

Schwartz, S., and Bone, M., *Retelling, Relating, Reflecting.* Toronto: Irwin Publishing, 1995.

Stahl, S. and Kapinus, B., "Possible sentences: Predicting word meaning to teach content area vocabulary" in *The Reading Teacher,* 45, 1991, pp. 36–43.

Strickland, D., *Teaching phonics today:A primer for educators.* Newark, DE: International Reading Association, 1998.

Strickland, Dorothy L., "What's Basic in Beginning Reading? Finding Common Ground" in *Educational Leadership,* 55:6, March 1998.

Taberski, S., *On Solid Ground: Strategies for Teaching Reading K–3.* Portsmouth, NH: Heinemann, 2000.

Tomlinson, Carol Anne, *The Differentiated Classroom: Responding to the Needs of All Learners.* Alexandria VA: ASCD, 1999.

Vygotsky, L.S., *Mind in society: The development of higher psychological processes,* M.Cole, V. John-Steiner, S. Scribner, and E. Souberman, eds and trans. Cambridge, MA: Harvard University Press, 1978.

Wagstaff, Janiel M., *Teaching Reading and Writing with Word Walls.* New York: Scholastic Professional Books, 1999.

Wylie, R.E., and Durrell, D.D., "Teaching vowels through phonograms" in *Elementary English,* 47, 1970, pp. 787–91.

CHILDREN'S BOOKS CITED

All Clean by Jo Winsor, illustrated by Richard Hoit; Rigby, 1999.

A Sun, A Flower by Sally Odgers, illustrated by Geoffrey Cox; Wright Group Publishing, 1997.

Baby Canada Goose Flies South by Janet Intscher, illustrated by Rebecca Buchanan; Curriculum Plus, 2001.

Mothers and Babies by Jennifer Low, illustrated by Effie Balmoenos; Curriculum Plus, 2001.

The Paper Bag Princess by Robert Munsch, illustrated by Michael Martchenko; Annick, 1988.

Sun Fun by Elle Ruth Orav, illustrated by Lam Quach; Curriculum Plus, 2001.

Tiger Catcher's Kid by Sylvia McNicoll; Nelson Canada, 1989.

The True Story of the Three Little Pigs by A. Wolf, as told to Jon Scieszka, illustrated by Lane Smith; Puffin, 1996.

Twilight Comes Twice by Ralph Fletcher, illustrated by Kate Keisler; Houghton Mifflin, 1997.

What a Story! by Paul Kropp, illustrated by Loris Lesynski; Scholastic Canada, 2002.

Index